PLANTATION AMERICA

Secrets of modern day slavery....

By Jack Freeman

Disclaimer

About the Author

In order to put this in prospective for the reader, there must be a little bit of a description of who the Author is and his qualifications to write such a book. The Author felt to write this type of book because of the current state of politics in the nation that really affect us all, rich and poor alike. Some people are just obviously more subject to suffer, and most of the time it is the people with less money in their pocket.

The Author was born in Los Angeles, California…

...he was raised and grew up in the small city of Marina Del Rey near the beaches of Venice and Santa Monica. Living in this area was an eye opener to the big differences in the country. There was actually lower income ghetto areas in Venice and Santa Monica , right side by side to extremely wealthy and affluent homes .Growing up it was obvious the discrimination the local police practiced by heavily patrolling the tiny ghetto areas and harassing the minority brown and black population. The crime rate in the poor areas did require some type of constant policing, but nonetheless the question still remained. What was the true cause of these great disparities in the community? And what were the root causes? Was this reality something that naturally came to exist, or was it a reality created artificially and intentionally by a sophisticated design? The author from the inside experience of harassment and false accusations from government officials was able to learn first hand the true nature of government and how it creates poverty, violence, and misery in certain communities. As unbelievable as it seems at first, these awful conditions are purposely created through sophisticated and indirect means that foster and breed a separation between the people in the form of rich and poor, where violence is provoked and encouraged for the poor. The government, using gross and unspeakable methods such as provoking gang wars and dumping huge amounts of drugs in the targeted areas, such as was confessed by the government in the "Iran-Contra" scandal, where congressional investigations revealed it, purposely bring about the conditions of misery now present in the ghetto areas. In turn individuals in government in the highest levels, profit through multi-national corporations by extracting revenue from these affected areas in the form of private prison ownership profiteering, drug rehabilitation centers, psychiatric drug prescriptions and other devious and discreet means, that are also designed to perpetuate this treacherous cycle in America.

Having spent time in county jails and in prisons and dealing with the legal court system directly as his own attorney , many disturbing but true facts where learned from law books, jury trial experience and directly from the mouth of judges and prosecutors. The corruption extends to the highest levels of government, and even then there is still much hope to create a better place for all of us to live in. All the undesirable experience of the author might seem to propose a biased and disgruntled point of view from where to speak from. But on the contrary the author keeps in mind the intention to give a fair point of view even in the light of all the unhappy and damaging facts that are presented within this book. Having both experienced poverty and wealth, the point of view here comes from a position of attempted total understanding, with the aim of provoking a complete, honest, and most of all truthful discussion amongst all people to bring about a fair, equal and love filled world. It might seem impossible at times, but then again mankind has repeatedly conquered the impossible in the pages of history. The author believes an amazingly beautiful and abundant experience for the entire world is a real attainable goal.

The Author

January 6, 2013
San Bernardino County Newspaper

= The Sun =

By Ben Boychuk

Consent is key. Americans are much less willing to trust their government today than they were even a generation ago. In August 2011 a Rasmussen Reports survey found that a pitiful 17 percent of likely U.S voters believed "Federal government today has the consent of the governed". Another pollster democrat Pat Cadell called the result "unprecedented…"

Introduction

Plantation America, will introduce you to the concept of Liberty, Freedom and what is that we have truly lost by not paying attention to what freedom really is. Government has once again been transformed into a machine that oppresses the people, a machine that is at this moment the method of imposing slavery upon the people on this land known as the united states of America. Once again the people are literally the property of the slave master , according to the law of the Land, as you will come to see as you read Plantation America. Rich and poor alike are the subjects of the kingdom, but this kingdom does not have a king in open view for the people to see, instead the king hides his face behind the many arms of control, such as the local court house, city hall, and the California and United States Supreme Courts. The soldiers of the king are your local police department and sheriff department implementing the will of the king by brute an unnecessary Force in many instances. As far fetched as it may sound or as hard as it might be to except- we have been conquered by the enemy. The most shocking aspect of this slavery, is the fact that, we the people are actively guilty of aiding and abetting the modern day slavery. Our lack of knowledge of the process of creating laws and how it is that they apply to any one of us, is the primary cause of this transformation from free people to slaves, in this "land of the free and home of the brave". As you read Plantation America you will be exposed to irrefutable truths, facts that you will be able to verify. These facts will cause you to get feeling of disbelief that it cant be so, but no matter how you feel, these verifiable facts will demonstrate to you the truth of what you would never believe. The truth is that we are all lied to by government agents, we have trusted these agents and we have been deceived into giving up our property, our rights, and our freedom most of all.

By clever design our government agencies have been separated into different departments, offices, and positions, therefore allowing our own fellow neighbor to be the king's arm of oppression with out even knowing what they are really doing. In this clever design we actively work to enslave ourselves and our children without ever feeling the guilt of our fault.

Today we have modern day slavery in America. You do not have to believe it, but you do have to live it. Attempt to truly live free, by for example not paying income or property tax and you will find yourself entangled in a legal battle for your freedom and or fruit of your labors such as your money, home, or other possessions. Sure some so called "tax protesters" manage to win in court, but only after long drawn out legal battles that emotionally and financially consume and drain its target victims and these are very few that dare take on the mind control puppets of the Slave master. The mind controlled puppet as you will see in "Plantation America" are your friends and neighbors, it might even be you. By this epic and magnificent design, people are separated into specialized and isolated positions within this mental slave plantation. Where everybody is "just doing their job" and without noticing is participating in a grand collective scheme that implements this modern day slavery. A great system is to combine this complicated and intricate design with the internal attack on our minds by tampering with the food supply and subliminal programming used in television and the music industry, and you have the most effective slavery in the history of the world. Where violence is used as last resort because people voluntarily comply. Behold the matrix is where you live. From the beginning of this "country" and "state" the plans to enslave the masses have been carefully carried out by the "Founding Fathers" and before even them. Here the nets of slavery are revealed , one by one, your mind will put together the mental image as you read through chapter after chapter and learn these invisible ropes and chains called , citizenship , traffic citations, taxes ,jurisdiction ,the constitution and other lofty tittles given to the power exercised over the people.

The most convincing Marketing you have ever seen unleashed is part of this sophisticated plan. As some people awaken to the fraud, the word is getting out. The most mysterious part of the unraveling of this scheme is the coming changes, and how will the people manage, if at all to re-organize. Will the people really manage to implement true freedom or will the people once again be tricked into slavery with nice labels meant to enslave the masses as has been done for thousands of year.

Table of Contents

Chapter 1

Creation of the "STATE OF CALIFORNIA"

In the beginning, the entity called "State of California" was just a new concept, a new idea to the state of a modern day Slavery Plantation, where once again the few wealthy and intellectual would hold the power over the masses of people. In 1849 some group of people, that were obviously wealthy and intellectual, put together a written document called the "Constitution for the State of California". This document was offered to the People in the geographical Land mass area known as "California", at the time. This document called the "Constitution "was an invitation for the people to vote for the new government structure. Who exactly offered this structure to the people is not exactly known, but we can guess to who financed this proposition as not many were in position to do so. This constitution offered a chance for people to vote "For the Constitution" or vote "Against the Constitution", according to Article 12 section 6 of this proposed Constitution . The elections were set to be held in November of the year 1849. According to the document this Constitution was proposed by the existing government structure. This structure was nothing more then men in certain positions with jobs to perform some function for the public. Most likely their power was exercised through imposing their will with violence or threat of it. Through some type of position that exercised power much like a sheriff or police officer does now a days. The rules of society are written called "Laws" and there is men appointed and guns given to them to enforce these so-called Laws.

The constitution of 1849 apparently was vote into power, and instantly created an entity called "State of California". In turn it created all these new government positions such as the "Governor" the "Legislature" and a whole bunch of other positions. These office positions were filled and a new government was up in operations. By operations I mean the rule of violence started. A beautifully ingenious plan to turn people into slaves and at the same time fool them into thinking they were free people to live as they choose. We here in the Country called the United States of America, still refer to this nation as "The Land of the Free and home of the Brave", even though it is anything but the land of the "Free" or home of the "Brave". Without going through the entire document called the "Constitution" in detail to prove this point, we will just get straight to the point and prove the fraudulent intention and greatest lie in the entire document. Article 1, section

1 of this document called the "Constitution" it states the following in plain and simple English:

"Sec.1 All men are by nature free and independent, and have certain inalienable rights, among which are those of enjoying and defending life and liberty, acquiring, possessing, and protecting property: and pursuing and obtaining safety and happiness."

Now if we analyze this statement, or section, or article, or whatever fancy name or title we apply to this grouping of words, we can see the biggest lie ever. It states that "All men are by nature free and independent". The reason that this is the biggest lie in the document designed to entice people to accept people to except this document as their law, is because at the time this document was proposed, 1849, there was much discrimination and inequality in the land exercised by the "white" inhabitants of the land. Now, maybe this document was going to put an end to this type of behavior, this type of unequal treatment amongst the people of the land of different races. Such as the wars between the "whites" and the "Native Americans" for possession of certain parts of the land. As it is well known that the men in government at those times were constantly attacking other men with violence and killing fellow men, of different races, for the simple reason non-other then they were attempting to steal the land from each other through violent means.   White men or men of European origin were generally the ones that were the aggressors, in return the Native Americans behaved the same way. So at first glance at reading this document you would think that there was about to be a big change in the approach the drafters of this document were using.   But before we can finish the document we start to see the same pattern of exclusion of certain types of people from this new proposed "State", or government structure. In Article 12 of section 5 of this proposed Constitution we can see the continuation of the Division of the races, which in part states that:

"Every citizen of California, declared a legal voter by this constitution,…..,"

so here we have a section of this document that is opening the door for the continued discrimination amongst the people of the land. This provision is basically allowing for some group of men   that is part of the government establishment to start to say who is and who is not "Free and Independent". Further to the point, where the racism gets very clear is in section 1 of Article 2 which begins with   the words:

"every white male citizen of the United States, and every white male

citizen of Mexico,….."

goes right to reveal the nature of this document, that "All people" are not free and independent in the true sense of the plain English language.

So this document starts with a lie, a false statement that through the document is twisted into a worthless statement with no effect after being neutralized and qualified out of existence. How can "All people be free and independent ….", when the document goes on to mention that "white" people are recognized but other people are not. It clearly implies that black people and other non-white people are not declared legal voters. Only some people can participate in this "Constitutional" government.

I guess this is just part of the progress of people into a more "Fair" or "Free" country as we all hope for. After all this is the California Constitution of 1849, not the one of 1879 as amended through the years and which we currently operate the state of California. The current constitution the state operates has removed racist descriptions from it. It is actually very different that the original constitution of 1849. The only section that is almost the same as today's version is Article 1 section 1. The section that says this state government recognizes that "All men by nature are free and independent ….", the foundation of the deceptive mind control on the people of this state.

But as we all come to see and learn the wording of racism has been removed. Other sections have been added to speak of "equal protection" and things in that nature. So the wording has been sanitized, it has been refined to a more acceptable display for words, but the effect is the same. To enslave, and manipulate the people into submission. Unfortunately we get to see the truth as we analyze and dissect the details of the written "Law" and the actual reality that is imposed on the people living in this great state and nation. As this story unfolds in our investigation of this present government you began to see not only that the people have been fooled into voluntarily going along with the lies, the government encouraged racism and discrimination , but that those individuals that do not go along with the state sponsored stealing, terrorizing , and murdering of people will be violently silenced and made to be quite about any type of criticism of failed policies or laws that they do not agree with or feel are unjust and need to be spoke up against . Just follow any protest in any big city. Such as the peaceful "occupy wall street" or other such similar protest, you will see that soon enough the police start to fire off tear gas or some type of light weight violent weapon. In any event at the minimum the police start to push up on the protesters to provoke ant type of reaction, so then the police can feel justified in the following assault on the people, and in the end the police claim the protesters got violent. When in reality the police provoke the violence either directly or indirectly. History and declassified documents from the government almost always come to reveal that the government had infiltrated these peaceful protest groups to incite violence or to persuade the unsuspecting members of these groups of citizens that are looking for peaceful change to the laws, instead provoke violence.

But before we get ahead of ourselves, we need to look at the foundation of the society we cal "government", the "State of California" , "country", or "nation". The foundation or the basis from where the power comes from is what exposes the true purposes of government. As history will clearly show, mankind has been evolving in technology, science, and in its mentality towards a more peaceful approach in living. At least in this nation called America. Because as we can see on a world wide scale countries and governments are still constantly at war with each other for whatever trivial excuse. On a worldwide scale there are many conflicts that are obviously man made. Some countries we might assume are not civilized, and that is why America must resort to war, but if that was true then the more civilized and advanced nation don't have open wars against each other but this is mostly because advanced nation have the ability to defend themselves through world devastating nuclear weapons. So what big advanced nations do instead is show their true mindset by using advanced military strength to wage brutal war against undeveloped nations that are pretty much unable to defend themselves. This behavior of using deadly violence against the inhabitants of small and defenseless nations is just a reflection of what the high level government officials believe is an acceptable behavior towards people that can't defend themselves. High level government officials in America have the same approach to the people of this country, but they must strike in subtle and non-obvious ways or else the people might try to have them arrested and removed from office. But either way the government's intension to control through violence is evident.

Here in America the government was allegedly formed for the purpose of protecting the people and securing the liberties and rights of the people living in the nation. The government is supposed to be a government of "We the People". The words "We the People" are all over documents that formed this government. There is even a court case where judges recognize the source of power is the "People" of this nation. Then there is even statutes , or laws, that are in the law books of each state that recognizes who the authority is in the country is and where the authority is supposedly derived from. We will look at California for example. In California we have what is called the California Government Code, which has some of the laws that apply supposedly to people and government in this state. In this "Government Code", sections 100, 100(a), 100 (b), the law or code or whatever fancy name is used to refer to this "rule", clearly states a few words that "Sovereignty resides in the people", and that all prosecutions are in the name of and by the authority of "The People". I'm not going to say what it means legally or otherwise, but I will let the reader decide. Then we have this other simple sentence in the California Constitution in Article 2 section 1:

"All political power is inherent in the people"

So with out me telling anyone what it means or getting into legal definitions or arguments about these statements in law. I'm sure one thing all the people that are not attorneys and don't have education in law can agree on, is that it certainly does imply the people have some type of position in the government structure. The more we look into the "law" such as codes or court rulings made by judges of appeal courts or Supreme Courts , the more we see the same pattern of statements that imply the "People" have some type of authority or power in the actions of the government. Of course the study of law is complicated and not easy, but it is in English language. At least for the most part, therefore it would be fair to say that a non-lawyer would be able to understand it after sometime of studying the law. There is no need to quote all types of laws or court rulings, everyone knows it is generally known that this is a "Free" country. Or so we are told from many different sources for the most part we have also heard the phrase "Land of the Free, Home of the Brave". The point is the people of this land are led to believe through many statements or sources that the people that inhabit this land known as America, are "Free" people. Whoever puts together this propaganda is quite clever. But is this propaganda that is really intentionally written to mislead the people of the land? But who would do something like that and how is it possible? Not only does it sound like some way out conspiracy, but it would have to be exactly that, a way out conspiracy to accomplish such a vast enslavement of the people through massive deceit.

Chapter 2

Freemasons

If we look at the history of who were the signers of the Declaration of Independence were, or if we look at the architecture of the older government buildings, specifically in Washington D.C, we begin to find some answers. These buildings in Washington D.C have some very interesting symbols and designs that were put there purposely by the designers of these old government buildings. A group of people known as the Freemasons have been written about heavily in books. The Freemasons are still active today as it is visible that meeting centers are in almost all big towns across America. The Freemasons are said to have a heavy influence in the creation of the government of this country , and it is true from the federal all the way down to the local state and county levels .Freemason are a type of public but secret society. Public in the sense that the Freemason as an organization is well known to exist as a member lodges nationwide. It nonetheless is a secret society because it is a society, or organization that is known for secrecy in its complete functions and purpose. In Ballentines Law Dictionary the third edition it is defined as an organization that is charitable in nature sometimes and other times not. What is very significant is that the word "Freemason" is to be found defined in a law dictionary, which is supposed to be a dictionary for legal terms used in legal writing such as law books and court rulings. This gives a hint that the Freemasons must have some kind of significant involvement in the law or the structure of the government itself. Freemasons have been accused of many things and most of the times it is just that, accusations. But instead of speaking of rumors that are not proven to be true and are just speculations, we can simply focus on what is fact. It is a fact that many old structures were designed and or financed by the Freemasons. It is fact based on many of these building have placards or engraving on the buildings themselves. All over downtown Los Angeles, there is such buildings. Across the street from the Kodak Theater in Hollywood, California is also a building with such a placard of metal built onto the concrete building. Most significant is the Government building in Washington D.C. The Freemasons mark is everywhere in Washington D.C The other most visible and widely known Freemasonry symbol is that of the one dollar bill in America, and many books have been written about George Washington and his involvement in freemasonry . This organization from the looks of it and the fact that it has survived hundreds of years to this present day, most likely seems to be able to have influenced and still be influencing politics today. Many politicians today are said to be part of the Freemason organization. Hundreds of books have been written on the Freemason and their alleged activities in America.

If any group of people could be organized the creation of the government such as the state of California, of other states and of the Federal government, it most certainly could have been the Freemasons. After all the Freemasons put their mark and symbols on many government buildings, and it is widely known that only the founding fathers were open participants in freemasonry. In the time of the creation of the states such as California, it was known that only the wealthy were allowed to be Freemasons. Or you had to be of high intelligence to belong. Most likely high intelligence came from higher education, this type of education was only available to the wealthy or to the favored and indebted to the wealthy. In these times there was an astronomical gap in the sophistication of the mind of the average population and the wealthy families. Wealthy families throughout history have ruled nations, and industries, and the same can be said of today's nations and industrial economic powers. The only difference is that today we are more distracted by events in life, such as wars and television soap operas, and other created distractions, not to forget sports like football and baseball. Governments don't fall apart and crumble because there is most likely someone pulling the strings from behind the scenes. Just like the corporations such as "McDonalds" or "Homedepot" is owned by its shareholders, so is the government owned by its shareholders. Yes, that is the same exact structure and method utilized by the rich and wealthy to own and run the government. So is the government a corporation? Yes, it surely is. The Federal government is a corporation, as encoded and clearly states in Federal Law. The states are corporations also. The information can be found in any Public Law Library in every county of the state. All local government agencies are even corporations by the government s own written laws. All the way down to most cities. On the city level you can find this fact written on city vehicles sometimes or city government stationary and or seals. Such words as "Incorporated in 1908" or some other year, have been seen on many a city property. So on the city level it is evident that cities are corporations without having to visit the local Law Library and do intensive research . Most people see no big deal that a government is a corporation. But a close analysis of this fact reveals some troubling reasons why a corporation is not good for the people, even when a corporate structure is great for the owners or shareholders. First let's get something clear. The people controlled by this government corporation are not the shareholders . Not only are the people of the nation not it's shareholders or owners, the people of the nation and states have absolutely no right to know who the shareholders or owners of the government corporations are. The shareholders own and direct the corporate government departments and entities which direct people's lives. The wealth of profits and revenue is transferred from the corporation's public bank accounts to the private personal bank accounts of its owner shareholder. The only thing the corporation does get to keep is the huge amount of debt that is amounting every year. The debt is presented to the unsuspecting citizenry as a reason to raise taxes and shut down much needed services and raise interest rates on loans and mortgages. A very ingenious way to "steal" people's property and oppress the masses. Sounds like a big conspiracy, but it is really a fact of life. Just think about it. How can the debt of the nation go up every year, when the government just prints pieces of paper as they desire. The whole claim of having a trillion dollar debt is a big joke.

As we see , the Freemasons as a secret society , and a wealthy one at that made up of intellectuals could have easily accomplished this grand scheme of enslaving the people . The most interesting part of this scheme to enslave the people is that people are easily duped because of my reasons but mostly the people's tendency to be lazy to learn for themselves the true nature of government and of their "jobs" within the government . Can we believe that the founding fathers as Freemasons would be that evil, or could it be maybe the founding fathers as Freemasons were just not as freedom loving as they claimed to be. For example, the Declaration of Independence made statements of freedom and equal rights, of making people free from the slavery imposed on them by the king of England at the time. The Declaration of Independence was said to be inspired and penned by of all people, Thomas Jefferson .At the time it was written and for many years after, slavery was openly a respectable trade by these founding fathers. So we have Thomas Jefferson talking of equality amongst men, freedom for all, and the love of our God. Yet at the same time these founding fathers are speaking of freedom for all and condemning tyranny and oppression by the king of England, the same founding fathers are slave masters, owners of thousands of slaves. Thomas Jefferson was widely known to own 1,000 of slaves and used them to build his home, work his fields, and cater to him hands and feet. And the female slaves he owned, we can imagine. Basically slavery was Thomas Jefferson livelihood. These Freemasons employed whatever method to manipulate society to get the desired end results. The end result as we can see today is for a specific group of families to position themselves in a superior station of control over the nation. Maybe out of a sense of owner ship based on their organization of a national government .

Either way it does not change the fact . For some reason, even though it is publicly known that these Freemasons as they advocated freedom, at the same time were proud slave masters, no one bothers to see anything wrong with that. No one seems to question why this was so, and not many are willing to point out this controversial fact.

Freemasons are suspected of being in positions not only of government, but also of the media, and other positions of importance to control the flow of information. The majority of newspapers around the nation, periodicals, popular magazines, and most important TV news outlets, are said to be owned and run by the Freemasons of today. These people are known to further the interest of the organization through coordinated efforts. The prize appears to be money and power . The power allows more accumulation of money and material possessions. The organization is known to operate on a basis of levels of membership . From the level of apprentice to Grand Master. There are some 33 or more levels in the structure of the Freemasons. The lower levels of Freemasons have less knowledge and power of the secret society. As the recruits go up in rank through some unknown criteria, the recruits are exposed to more "secret" information which allows them to gain more material wealth. The higher ranks these Freemasons attain , the more access to resources that will increase their power and wealth. This information is assumed to be insider advanced information only available to member of this elite organization. Such things as approval of loans from banks for personal or business purposes, exemptions from criminal's prosecutions, no bid   contracts to cushy government contracts. Who can resist such opportunity to belong to such a powerful nationwide organization, if not worldwide. An organization known to be well respected, well funded, and very well established in government can offer anyone riches beyond their wildest dreams. Of course at the expense of the health and well being of those not within the organization . This is where the common population comes in, where without notice are deprived of a better existence through unbelievable and intricate design of control coupled with revenue extractions.

Freemasonry has long existed and is known to have come from European origins, where a selected few gathered together to share secret knowledge concerning the mason trade. From here these individuals saw the power in the collective organization of information not known to the general population. They were sought out by the wealthy and powerful elite of their time , by the kings and queens of the world to construct building for many purposes . Palaces , castles , cathedrals, and man famous places were designed and built by Freemasons. This demand for the Freemason's service brought an abundance in wealth for their secret knowledge. The Freemasons were said to posses the knowledge of "Sacred Geometry". This information enabled them to build structures of a grand scale that other could not. A lot of their structures still stand to this day as solid as the day they were built 500 to 1000 years ago. When modern day construction has crumbled in earthquakes or tornadoes, the old Freemason structures stand strong and unscathed. The organization from then on , from what appears began to collect and organized powerful information in different sectors of life, such as politics, medicine, food, nature, science and every field of information possible to become what they are today.

Freemasons have even been accused of being just evil in intentions. They have their own "Freemason Bible" and somewhat operate as a demonic religion. Although on the surface the organization appears to be charitable, a closer look at their operation starts to show an almost cult-like group. Members wear funny outfits and perform odd rituals that are spooky in nature. The rituals they perform are hundreds of years old in their customs, and give the members a sense of brotherhood and loyalty.

In order to run an organization like the Freemasons and accomplish such a goal as controlling the direction of people in a nation, there has to be a very exact power structure that is coordinated from somewhere. There must be rewards in material wealth for members in politics and more specifically the criminal legal system in America. This enables its members to be protected from exposure to criminal prosecutions or the detrimental power of the news media that can bring any organization to its knees through popular opinion of the people.

There is said to be other secret societies within the Freemason organization which from power structures within this society. The same pattern emerges when we look into these societies. A pattern of wealthy individuals in positions in big corporations that have a big influence in the shaping of public opinion to sway elections to the favor of the super wealthy, in order for the majority of the population to be led down a life of true information blackout. This control of information in the nation concerning such industries as food, agriculture, medicine, news, media of all starts, entertainment, education in general, money, finance, real estate, banking, drugs- legal and illegal, law, the political process, and any other vital area of information concerning the mental state of reality required to form and maintain a particular status quo. The control of a nation is no easy task, therefore we must look at the tiniest detail in order to figure out how this structure maintains its control amongst such people in such people in a free and open society. Or what we believe to be a free and open society. On the surface of laws and related documents it seems there is nothing wrong, on the contrary, everything sounds good. The only way we can determine if Freemasons really have anything to do with controlling anything in this country, is to dig deep into information with an unbiased prospective. In order for anyone to do this effectively, they must be very informed about the media, politics, history, the main industries supporting the economy, banking, finance, and the individuals that are involved. These people are inter-related in one way or another, they even casually form groups and associations without raising any eyebrows of the people. They effectively hide behind secret partnerships by using the professional veil of a corporation. Its just business as usual in America. While the people look, but do not see, the intricate web of a real life conspiracy is really happening everywhere in every important part of daily life.

These organizations including the Freemasons have rituals they perform on a regular basis. They also have rituals they perform to enter into the organization and become members .Although they don't claim to be religious, they very closely operate as religious. They use symbols and drawings that identify with some people would associate with "Satanism" or what is known as evil religions, but members openly in public deny that these societies are demonic or evil in anyway. The members would also clearly deny that participate in any human blood sacrifice or any such related criminal activity. The most obvious reason is the criminal liability that could put these people in jail for such behavior. We really don't know exactly what these secret societies do. For the most part because of the fact that they do behave secretly. Some activities are public , but not many at all. Members will say they cannot divulge secrets of the organization . The question is why? Why so many secrets? Of course everyone is entitled to privacy in this country. But an organization that is so huge and known to have over 5 million members in America, and has so many high level government members, does raise some suspicion. Especially when you consider the fact that for hundreds of years these organizations have been accused by many people of participating and forming conspiracies in this country and abroad.

A member in the millions in any type of society is powerful force. Whether it be for good or bad purposes. One thing for sure is that, this type of group can make a difference in any activity they get involved in. And it can be very unfortunate if this group were to be involved in any type of conspiracy or behavior that oppresses the people of this land. To this date Freemasons are as American as apple pie, they are pretty much the structure in the shadow that shapes the direction of the government. It all started by who we have heard are called the founding fathers.

Chapter 3

Founding Fathers

From what is taught in local schools and according to established history. Whether it be true or not, there was a hand few of significant people that established the basis of this government. Which is interesting in itself, since this is supposed to be a government of "we the people" which implies "the people" would have had a role other than to vote to accept or deny a proposed government structure, that was designed by a selected few. Even if we look at the most recent framework that this government operates under, the California Constitution of 1849 as amended to date, there was not of a creative role by "the People". Under the present form of government, which operates under what is called a constitution "the People" did not have much of a role in creating the government either. Nor did they get to choose to operate under a "constitution" or "Federation", " the People" basically had no role in the design of the government. As explained in the first chapter of this book, this document called a "Constitution" was presented to "the People" of the land to either vote " For" or "Against" the constitution. We were told according to the officially approved history, that there were

"Founding Fathers" to this nation. These people debated and drafted the documents that are the basis for today's government .

"Founding Fathers" include men like Benjamin Franklin, George Washington, and Thomas Jefferson. There of course were others, but these were the most notably recognized by history text books. These men are all well documented to have belonged to the secret society known as the Freemasons. This society was a popular society in those days that was well known to accept only the upper or middle white class of men in their time. The average working man in those times was not very educated in a formal sense concerning history and or the workings of the government. Schooling was not a luxury afforded to the public in general as it is today. Therefore the wealthy schooled the intelligent men of those times were at a great advantage to easily create a government. Not only could they create a government on paper through their superior intelligence, they could actually organize and enforce it upon the less intelligent and poor. The mental capacity to create and organize a government was easily available to these Freemasons. The physical ability to impose and enforce this Freemason designed government was there also. To enforce this scheme on an entire population of such great scale would require vast amount of financial resources to acquire other material resources to force these rules called

"Laws" onto the people. A central government structure had to be created with many outposts to coordinate the control of this new kingdom. The Founding Fathers had devised a plan to impose their will on the "People" of the land. These Freemasons pooled their financial and intellectual resources to create this new type of kingdom . In this new design of kingdom, there was no king with concentrated power. This modern kingdom was created by a group of men that decided to share evenly the spoils of war. The prize to them was the fruit and the labor of the common man. The power was shared and distributed amongst these Freemasons, with the power and possessions preserved for their posterity when they would die. The evidence of this is in the present day government. The most powerful corporations and or legal entities in this country are still in control of the countries direction. Just like a king would pass the throne to his sons for generations. Such as the Queen of England inherited her kingdom from her bloodline without any vote or consent, but is merely tyranny in a disguise. The people either agree with the king's rules or they are violently beat and captured like wild dangerous animals. The voting process is just basic mind control so the people have the illusion of having rights or a say so in current government politics. More of this will be proven by facts in later chapters.

Kingdoms as history has clearly proven are nothing more than cleverly designed slave plantations. Even for those that don't agree and have lived somewhat comfortable in a kingdom, there is one indisputable fact. That is a kingdom not congruent with freedom. The people are subjects of the king. Kingdoms are not the most popular places to live for many people. History proves this. When America Land became known of by the people of faraway kingdoms, the subjects of those kingdom fled by the boat loads to America. Even the wealthy or privileged that lived well within the kingdoms left. It was not just the poor and oppressed that dashed out of these kingdoms as fast as possible. The rich, wealthy and intellectual run away and escaped these kingdoms just as fast if not faster then the lower classes. This historical fact says volumes about people's opinion of living in a kingdom under a king with such a power structure of classes and inequality. No matter how privileged some people were allowed to live in an unfair prison known as a kingdom , the privilege still left when a land or location became available where people could possibly live free and govern themselves. Or so they were told . Either way we look at it, just the prospect of living a life outside of a kingdom where more freedom and more fair life was available, all peoples of all types, fled there.

These Founding Fathers according to history congregated and exchanged ideas for the supposed   benefit of bettering mankind. Text books claim these meetings called "Conventions" and by other fancy names were for the purpose of securing all peoples freedom and god given rights. These god-given rights were named inalienable rights within documents such as the now-famous "Declaration of Independence " and have survived to the present day in Article 1 section 1 of the California Constitution . At least the illusion has. The founding fathers themselves were nothing more than intellectual snake-oil salesman . They came up with a creative story of freedom for all people and a land of the "free". When in reality through the actions of these founding fathers we see they valued something else above all. These founding fathers really coveted the powers of the former king under which they lived under. Their actions clearly reveal their true intentions. We don't even have to dig to deep to find this incriminating evidence. It is well known and undisputed that George Washington and Thomas Jefferson owed their entire wealth to the fact they owned slaves. They financially gained at the expense of reducing another living man to the status of a slave. These men of so called respectable stature that claimed it was "Self-evident" that all men were created equal, housed people like a farmer house pigs and cattle. Slaves that tried to escape this captivity, were known to have their hand or feet cut off as a punishment if caught. Slaves were violently beat if they did not follow instructions from their "Masters". The founding fathers in there lust for power became tyrants, slave masters, racist bigots, and every other repugnant quality detestable to true freedom . Their mouths spoke words of true freedom , even the documents they provided and wrote reflected their spoken ideas of creating a true free country where all people are equal and fairness would provide a better quality of life for all people regardless of color. The real impact of the founding fathers behavior was the total opposite, totally unrecognizable to the idea of liberty. As day in and day out until their deaths, they ran slave plantations that doubled as their private home. So as they sat at their desk writing documents boasting of freedom and their respect for mankind, they looked out the window to make sure their slaves plowed the fields as instructed, to secure their financial means of living.

The founding fathers set in motion this deceitful scheme that is still being perpetuated on the people of the land. Of course in a more modern method, and in a more safely covert manner. It's true that slavery no longer exists in its prior form, but it certainly does exist in a modern form. The biggest difference is that today it's more sanitized and it applies to all races above all. Before ,chains and whips were used to control the slave population. Today it is done with more subtle methods such as the use of taxes, imposing rules on what people can consume and so on. For example, your choice to drink whole milk straight from the cow is against the "Law". Regardless if your research in science and medical literature leads you to believe it's healthier and safer. To bad. You must follow the "Law" or a fine will be levied against you and your property seized if you don't pay . Seizing your property is done through "Legal Process", which basically is the government sending you a threat to pay or have your hard earned property taken by gun toting agents. So you voluntarily pay or it will be taken by force and violence, even if you must be violently beaten or shot and killed. And don't try to resist or you will be labeled a criminal and be blamed by the media for resisting and getting yourself killed. The same scenario can play out for not paying your taxes on your property. So what if you paid for your property in full. Every year you must pay a "Tax". This tax is suppose to be owed for services provided to you, even if you do not want the services offered. The best part is that if the service is not provided to you and your taxes have been paid, you can seldom if ever sue the government for breach of this forced contract. There is a multitude of court cases that proves this cold fact. Of course there is every one out of 400,000 cases where the "Citizen" , successfully sues the government , and this is methodically blasted on the television and newspapers to give the appearance to the people that there is rights and justice in this country. A strategic method to impose the slavery on the people. Or how about city codes that tell people what color you can paint your fence, or even determines how tall your front fence around your house can be? These are just a couple of small and very trivial issues that on the face appear non-significant. But the true nature of the beast called government is exposed if people do not voluntarily comply. The government exposes itself for what it really is if the people do not voluntarily comply. Behind all the soft and professional sounding words used by governments, is a brutal and violent slave master that that will collect its fine for your fence being built against the "Law", called a city code. Of course there are many layers before it gets there, but it will get there if the slave resists. A fine as such will cause a chain of events to set in motion if not paid, these events will continue until the fine grows by late fees into an amount that will eventually effect the credit rating of someone costing them money. Basically, strategic and convert methods of taking someone's property without confrontation, but no matter how you look at it, your gonna pay. A lien on a home for unpaid fines to the city is more direct, and can cause the city to sell your home if left unpaid for so long. Guess what, if you don't get out of the home when it is sold at auction from under you, the local sheriff will come to the property and physically remove you. Once again, we get the violence. If the sheriff has too, and you don't voluntarily leave, the swat team will show up, and if you get killed for resisting the extraction of your body from the property, then you are the criminal for not following the law.

As we look close at the behavior of the founding fathers, we begin to see the pattern of tyrant in disguise. The founding fathers basically developed and implemented a structure of control based on the control structure of a Corporation. It's a very hard truth to swallow, but it doesn't change the facts. By the documents such as the "Declaration of Independence", there must have been a sense of progress amongst the local common people concerning the whole concept of government. Especially with the title sold to the people, of a government "By the People". The words "We the People ", where used in a very convincing manner to subliminally get the common people of the land to believe that everyone would have some kind of controlling say-so in the construction or operation of the government. Therefore there was this understanding within the general population that they would basically govern themselves. That they would set their own rules by which to live. These methods which either intentionally used to mislead the people into this new form of Dictatorship by a group, or the founding fathers where oblivious to the true outcome of this form of government. Considering the fact that these Founding Fathers were extremely intelligent men in there time and were able to articulate with very refined skill, we must come to the conclusion that the new advanced method of dictatorship that was the outcome of their actions, was that of calculated intension. Just like in a modern day court where a criminals prior convictions are brought up in a trial to prove a character trait, we can look to these founding fathers character traits to determine their intention.

These Founding Fathers were known as Freemasons. They belonged to this organization that had and is still has a reputation of secrecy. The Freemason organization to this day is considered a secret society. Today the Freemasons are what the courts would refer to as a "gang". This "gang" was known to have allegedly participated in many conspiracies that involved everything from Bribery to Murder. Although these allegations might not have been proven, the fact that the Founding Fathers where gang members of a very powerful, if not the most powerful organization, makes them suspect. Paired with readily available information about them, such as the fact that they were all cold-hearted slave owners, totally puts their characters in a light of conniving liars. Once again traditional text books in public schools have mysteriously avoided any emphasis on this subject.

Of course this new form of Government did bring some type of progress to the concept of freedom and to some people under the new government of "We the People". Comparing it to the old system of government from under the kingdoms of Europe, it was a big leap towards a better quality of life. But very importantly we must not forget that the European kingdoms of government were not the only options available for structure of people to live by. We must remember that there were many people that lived on this land we call America , with functioning structures for the people. Whether these are better systems for the people to live by, seems very likely. It was a well known fact that many Europeans went to live in Native Indian Settlements in preference to the European styled colonies and settlements established at the time that the colonies were in existence. For some reason Europeans that come to America decided that the structure by which the Native Americans lived by was a better set of rules to live by. Obviously the European structure, even under the 13 colonies that supposedly governed themselves, had some type of undesirable attributes to it.

Even with the new positive points of this new government of "We the People", it is still a structure that is designed with the intention to impose a Dictatorship on the people. A Dictatorship through the rule of group instead of an individual. But this Dictatorship is like no other in the History of Mankind. It is a system that imposes slavery in a very covert method. Using indirect methods, and most importantly is the use of creative wording that fools the peoples mind at first glance. By using words such as Freedom of this and that, rights, equal protection, and the concept of voting for "Laws". No matter how you look at it, if the majority votes to take the property of someone that has the desire to drink pure milk instead of processed milk with a bunch of chemical additives, the people who are in the majority are imposing their belief and will on another without any authority. Just because they believe you shouldn't drink pure milk because you might get sick. A sickness that even if does happen will not spread and only effect the person drinking pure milk. This is the same as putting someone in jail or taking their property or punishing them for eating candy bars for breakfast, lunch, and dinner. Yes, it might be true that it's not very healthy, the person's stomach might hurt, they will probably get sick, and their teeth will certainly suffer some cavities. But this is a personal choice that will only physically injure the individual. To regulate and control some ones life in such a manner and use violent incarceration in a cage or warehouse as punishment is pure slavery. It is not slavery as practiced in the 1800's but it certainly is slavery in a more modern and futuristic way. At first it might not appear as slavery of any kind, until we look at the details and closely analyze such an experience someone might go through. Picture someone in a jail cell for drinking pure milk, against the laws of the state. As days go by deprived of their liberty, while their family and loved ones wait for the individual to be released. Is this just? Depends who you ask. Politicians would say yes, the victim in jail would say no. Any rational individual you would think would disagree with that type of punishment for that kind of offense. In the light of what this country claims to be, "The Land of The Free", this surely cannot be.

The progress that people have made under this form of government in America, have been hard earned by the people. The government at almost every turn tries to prevent the people's progress towards Freedom. The people have to protest and organize and take issues up in the courts of the country, where government attorneys oppose the people's process. When this government is suppose to be the government of "We the People". Why would the government attorneys oppose the will of the population? Does the government agent represent "The People" as they proceed with blatant disregard for the peoples wishes? So who are the people in the category of "We the People ", they cannot really be the same "people ", that inhabit the land.

These Founding Fathers created a dictatorship where this ownership power is passed down to their family members and illusion of freedom is perpetuated as a tactic of maintaining the control of the kingdom over the people kept in slavery. And they will never tell. The stakes are too high. An Empire to be exact. All progress is slowed down by government, by drawn out legal battles that take years to settle, sometimes up to 10 years. So the people must endure years and ridiculous amounts of legal fees to pay attorneys to fight these cases. If the people run out of the 100 thousand or more of dollars that this process requires then they loose the case. A very unlikely scenario if the government is of "We the People". This is how the people have been learning the truth of this country, when they find themselves in the situation of having to buy the opportunity to beg the courts for their rights. Such as the right to drink, buy, and sell pure untreated milk from a cow that has not been injected with chemical hormones. There are many court battles going on where the people of the land are going to court right now, and spending huge amounts of money on attorney fees for many issues, that are basically simple personal choices, but the national government for some reason or another has determined that such behavior by the people is a threat to it's continued control over the people. The freedom and rights that the people have obtained over the years might appear to be great gifts that the present government system has provided for the people, but they really are not. The Founding Fathers and their posterity have put obstacles in every way possible on the road to these freedoms and rights exercised today in America. The persistence of the people is what has provided any rights and freedoms. The continued protest, sacrifices of families and finances, and sometimes it has cost people their life. In cases like that of Martin Luther King, John F. Kennedy, Abraham Lincoln, and groups such as the Black Panthers, the Brown Berets, and other peace parties, people have lost lives to stand up for what they believe in. In history all over the world in many kinds of control structures over the people, there has only been progress in Freedom for the common people through continued struggle and constant pushing on the set limits imposed by the king, Tyrant, Dictator, or group of individuals that exercise power over the masses of people. This country has proven no different in the required struggle for progress. The only difference is the type of structure and path to obtain progress.

This government structure is designed through the most advanced thinking possible to impose total slavery in a modern way. This slave plantation called America, or the United States, or any combination of such words, is the same ugly beast of a dictator in a costume of a beautiful dame.

When the dress is removed the scary body of illusion and control are quickly realized in the victims mind. The chains are invisible and the fences to the prison untouchable, but are more effective in controlling population than ever a dictator could have wished for in his most wildest dreams. The truth really is stranger than fiction. In reality there is less freedom today than at the start of this nation, country, or United States Corporation, whatever you want to call it, that started over 200 years ago. The technological advances in science and electronics, and many other industries has provided for the total control and surveillance of the people on this land. With flying satellites in orbit that can read the license plates on a car and Global Positioning tracking on every cell phone, the tools of slavery have changed to an invisible method instead of visible fence around the prison plantation or a chain around the neck of a captive slave.

Chapter 4

Greatest Marketing Plan

When then do so many people believe this country to be so great or so desirable to come move here to live? We should look at what is the attractive factor. Looking at how many people come to this country everyday to start a new life, we can see that the attractive factor is the marketing of the country across the world. The United States Corporation is a master of marketing and advertising principles. This government on a Federal level runs the most effective and greatest marketing plan in the world. First of all research shows that marketing and advertising techniques have a profound effect on the minds of the people. It is actually a form of hypnotism or mind control. In hypnotism people can be mentally programmed to think they are animals, or to think they are freezing cold or believe almost anything that the hypnotist tells them to believe once in a trance. So basically we need to know and realize what marketing and advertising is. A form of mind control, a form of hypnotism with a different name to keep the target victims unsuspecting that they are really targets of some attempt to control their minds, though the desires, want, feeling and thoughts of the mind and body. Anyone that doesn't think hypnotism is a very serious and advanced secret science, can simply look in a book store and read the stories of the research that has been conducted on hypnotism. It is actually pretty unbelievable and amazing as to how easily the mind of a person can be programmed to believe something. Some studies even show peoples eye color can be changed by simple suggestion, or a blister made to appear on the skin of someone by telling them they got burned. Marketing and advertising is the same technique in a slighter less effective way, but it is still a very effective method overall. Products and services that people do not really need are sold to them every single day. Woman and men are both known to have addictions to shopping for things they really don't need .

Advertising and marketing are powerful methods of control that people regard as harmless or insignificant. The U.S Government spends 100's of millions on studies concerning advertising, and that is nothing concerning the billions spent annually by the government on scientist salaries to study and further develop methods of mind control. Many books on government mind control and the tests done by the government on the unknowing population exists today. One such book is titled "Mind Control". This book tells of real mind control by the government for the purpose of serving the government, the catch is that the people mind controlled where not asked to give permission to participate. Essentially real live slavery in the most destructive and disgusting way. Most of the time if not every single time the government agency and perpetrators escape without any liability or accountability to the person victimized and used in the experiment. We have to remember that most victims of mind control don't know they are victims. Just how the hypnotism man does not see anything wrong with barking like a dog when he is in a trance of mind.

As we have seen here mind control, advertising, hypnotism, and marketing all fall in the same category. They are all vehicles and tools of controlling a population that is ignorant of the powerful effect of advertising. Whether the advertising is on a poster board on the side of a building or on television or through radio and music. Constant bombarding of the human senses ultimately renders the target a willing and voluntary participant in whatever behavior is suggested. In American big cities people are drowned of their own rational thoughts by marketing and advertising around every corner.

Government markets and advertises itself as promoting freedom. In America all the documents establishing the foundation of this government constantly speak of rights, freedom, equal protection of the laws, fair proceedings in court, and the people as the foundation of the government's power. The "Declaration of Independence" is taught in schools, the Constitution of the states and of the Federal Government are also promoted in a light of respect for the people and their freedom. While the whole time the government operates through opposite principles of such teachings of freedom. The laws of the country are based on deceit and are implemented with the appearance of fairness in mind, but are anything but fair. Holidays such as the Fourth of July are carefully designed to continue the fraud that there is Freedom in this country. The yearly celebration of Fourth of July keeps the reminder to the people of the country going, or more accurately it keeps the lie going.

<u>Chapter 5</u>

Modern Day Slavery

Slavery has always been a part of history in certain parts of the world. In some parts of the world it has just been more prevalent, even a respected and accepted occupation. That of course has been a very long time ago when people were more brutal and heartless in the attitude towards life. At least that is what we are led to believe in the common history books. Considering the progress of technology of electronics, medicine, science, health, communication, and the access to valuable information in general, you would think that progress in the treatment of people would have also progressed for the better in many ways. Unfortunately for some odd reason, there is one aspect of life that has not kept up with the evolution of technology. Modern day slavery is what exists in America today and in most parts of the world. Ironically the developed civilized nations are the ones that practice it in the most aggressive and brutal way. In light of advances in all aspects of life, there has been almost no significant steps towards the concept of interaction between people concerning what relation to control each others lives exist among people. No matter how modern or civilized government appears today, it does not escape the traditional method of ruthless violence for its base of power. Slavery in disguise. This government is said to derive its power from the consent of the governed. That fallacy is quickly exposed by a person not wanting to give consent to be governed, or tries to withdraw any express or implied consent. Modern day slavery is invisible to most people now a days here in America. Not because it is not there, but because people have come to accept present day government as a fact of life. Most accept this established status due to fear of telling themselves the truth of the involuntary nature of participation in a government that routinely murders and steals with impunity across the country. All in the name of "We the People", whoever these people might be. Because when government profits from any ventures or endeavors through stealing, murder, violence or otherwise, there is no check of dividends sent out to all the people of the country. The most interesting and telling part of the deceitful and conniving character of the government is the tendency to send a bill to the people of the country for its unauthorized and self-approved escapades performed. This bill is sent out to the people of the country in the form of a "tax". Taxes on income, property, or services are imposed on the people without their consent. These taxes are collected through many creative ways. Many times the name of this tax is even changed to be called a "fee", or "premium", or toll to use a road or cross a bridge. All methods are employed to extract the wealth out of people. It appears this method is the same as the " taxation without representation" that the English fled from in coming to this land to form a new form of government. The people have come full circle back to the unsatisfactory conditions that motivated the mass exodus out of Europe and England. The money powers of the wealthy families out of Europe that created the financial enslavement of people in the past are the same family structures that run the central bank today called the Federal Reserve.

The constant promotion of holidays like Fourth of July through mass media and government sanctioned days off of work are nothing more than government corporate advertising to keep people believing there is true freedom in this country. A close look at research concerning the discrimination in this country against minorities is one of many issues that show otherwise. The Los Angeles Police Department as a corporation uses the motto, "to protect and serve", but seldom does a month go by without a police officer getting accused of corrupt criminal activity. The police officers in big cities drive around town like predators instead of agents of the people that are there to "protect and serve". They behave as modern day agents of slave masters, by constantly and aggressively harassing people, and treating them as slaves on a big plantation. Big cities have been converted into prison camps. There are many city ordinances and other "laws" that are designed to allow the police to treat people as slaves. The police in big cities intentionally use the pretense of a possible violation of some law, or ordinance to harass people and put handcuffs on them. The fact that even when the police officer cannot claim someone broke a law to detain and question them, but just can simply claim the person "looked suspicious", as a reason to stop and harass them is proof that people are treated as slaves instead of people with rights and equal standing in society. In many cities across America police regularly set up check points and stop every single car that passes through looking for drunk drivers. These same check points have been ruled unconstitutional and against the law by the courts, but police departments continue to deploy these check points with blatant disregard for the law and court process. The only remedy is to file a law suit in court again, with ridiculous cost to pursue the lawsuit. In the meantime the government entities such as police and sheriff's continue to behave in unconstitutional ways. Technically breaking the law. Agents that are supposed to respect the law created by the "people". It might be true that these checkpoints can save lives and prevent drunk drivers from causing injury, but so can regular police work of patrolling the street and looking out for drivers swerving. That is the difference of the police serving the people as they should, and the police behaving like slave masters oppressing the people at their will. The difference between living in the city of a free country, and living in a city that has been converted into a prison camp. If there is no difference then the government would be justified in searching everyone's homes with no probable cause and taking everything from people that can potentially be used as a weapon such as cooking knives and other tedious items like flammable household cleaners or anything of that nature.

The government is known for encroaching on people's right a tiny bit at a time as to not raise any suspicious or strong opposition to the encroaching of theses rights. The cold and raw truth is that for the most part this encroachment is imposed by mostly government employees that are honestly oblivious to the ultimate outcome of their actions. Certain policies or directives might come from individuals that know what they are doing, but the lower level agents that are carrying out these directives don't even bother to think of the real result of such enforcement. Even when they do, police and sheriffs carry out these oppressive policies in violation to their oath of office based on fear and lack of true principles and integrity. These agents of the state have been rendered mere instruments of the King to oppress the people, because any officer that doesn't follow "orders" can easily loose his job. So when an officers sees he is being ordered to do something that goes against his oath of office he swore to defend the country, he must literally choose between his job or his moral integrity. The worst part of that type of predicament for any officer is that, following orders he gets to keep his job and gains a sense of unity with other fellow officers he works with, but if he was to choose to stand up for the oath of office he swore to, he would loose his job and pretty much gain nothing and would certainly loose a lot along with his job. That is where the unfortunate circumstances come about. Although this scenario would not be so if the majority of people in government were not so corrupt. At this point in this country the government is so involved in a criminal culture and corrupt mindset that it's to the point of almost no return. Correction would have to come from outside the government structure, basically from the non-government people in society.

Chapter 6

Fraud

Another rock in the shoe of the country that prevents government from walking straight is the scope of the fraud perpetuated on the people. As you begin to see the bigger picture develop as you read through this book, the daily fraud perpetuated by the government on the people will be easy to see. This fraud touches everyone in the nation, the poor and the rich. Except like always the poor take it the hardest from lack of financial resources to get through the storm. Many if not most interactions with the government are based on fraud and could never exist without the element of fraud involved. When the fraud is revealed many get upset and file lawsuits against the present government to no avail. Sometimes people find remedy to the fraud in the court system against the government. Mostly only in minor matters and in limited circumstances. Most of the fraud that the daily operations of the government are based on, are so elaborate and of unbelievably astronomical design that the people that do attempt to file a lawsuit concerning the matter, will find themselves embroiled in a uphill loosing battle. The reason is that this government is based on fraud as its strategy to exist. The fraud you will see is the type of fraud as defined clearly by the laws of this country.

Everything in this government's relation to the people is based on a so called contract. From the application to get an identification card or drivers license to the passport or even the way a social security number is issued and enforced against the people of this country. All these documents require people to sign something in order to receive them or use them. Anytime anyone signs anything that person is entering into an agreement with another entity. A signature is someone's private property that is given as a symbol of consent and or agreement. These documents are all basically contracts. Courts have always declared them to be contracts and the legal structure and nature of these documents make them contracts as defined by law.

The reason peoples signatures are required is because this government claims to operate on the consent of the people. To operate against the people or proceed in any way against the people would make this government a dictatorship that doesn't require peoples consent. In many minuscule or not to deep reaching instances the government does operate through consent and does respect the long established rules and laws that govern contracts in this country. Just don't expect constant respect for the laws regarding rights or rules regulating contracts. In contracts fraud is not allowed and fraud renders any contract void and not valid as soon as the victim points it out and speaks up on it. Which it should as it is not only common sense but also long established law that is clearly respected by the courts of this country. The only problem the courts have following this rule of contracts is when the contracts involve government contracts or contracts relating to an industry the government profits from. Many politicians invest in certain industries so the government interest in those industries is tainted.

Fraud is basically when someone lies. Lack of disclosure is also fraud in contracts. There is only a few different ways to commit fraud in contracts. Then there is the other most common method that the government uses to gain peoples consent. Besides fraud in the inducement of contracts, the most effective method next in line is to use violent force or threats of violent force if someone does not give their consent to a contract in the form of a signature. The violence or threat of it is usually directly obvious but sometimes it is indirect. Consent sometimes is even gained by just simply not leaving the victim any other choice or the victim will suffer damage, physical or financial.

In California the basic rules of contract are available for anyone to read and are in a book called the California Civil Code. This is where the official rules are and then there are secondary authorities on the subject written by law professors, such as in Brian Blum's book "Contracts: Examples and Explanations". Brian Blum's book on contracts gives details and examples for a better understanding.

Once a good understanding of contracts and the concept of fraud and related elements that render contracts invalid and void is attained, the fraud being perpetuated on the people is crystal clear. Basically, an agreement or contract must be totally by mutual, voluntary consent and there can be no elements of fraud, deceit, violence, threats, or any kind of menace or duress involved. If there is the contract is void or can be voided by giving notice to the other party. These are basic and well established principles in American courts.

Chapter 7

Citizenship Defined

The foundation of fraud, lies, and deceit goes to the very heart of the principles of this country. Citizenship in America is also based on fraud and lies. To have citizenship in America is to be a member of the political society of this country. The word citizen is defined in Ballantines Law Dictionary 3rd edition as a member in a political society. The courts in the United States also say this about what citizenship is. In the case of Luria v. U.S., 231 U.S. 9,22, the court had this to say:

"Citizenship is membership in a political society, and implies a duty of allegiance on the part of the member and a duty of protection on the part of the society. These are reciprocal obligations, one being compensation for the other."

So this is what the men that call themselves lawyers and or judges had to say concerning citizenship. These rulings or statements are sometimes overturned or changed, but in light of the fact that this is pretty much the same definition in the law dictionary, we can fairly presume this is a correct position as to the definition. This relationship between the citizen and society appears to be a contract, some form of agreement with reciprocal obligations to each other. One has the duty of allegiance and the other the duty of protection. It sounds good at first, even a pretty reasonable agreement at first thought. Without research or investigation into this so-called agreement we just might believe it to be true but then we have many instances where the government has "No" obligation to protect the individual citizen. As a matter of fact there are hundreds of cases where the courts have repeatedly stated in many different scenarios that the government has "no" obligation to protect the citizen. Anyone can go to the local law library and pull up cases stating such. Here I will include one case to demonstrate what the courts say and establish the fact that citizenship is based on fraud. In the case of Bowers v. Devito, 686 F.2d 616 the court very clearly states the following:

"The constitution is a charter of negative liberties; it tells the state to let the people alone; it does not require the Federal government or the states to provide services, even so elementary a service as maintaining law and order."

And for those that think this is an isolated incident or a rare occasion when the court says such a thing, go to the law library and look these types of cases up. You will come to see that it is a common sentiment and well established rule of law that the government has no "obligation" to protect or provide services to the citizens of the country. So the government has no obligation to the people that are the citizens, but the people that are citizens continue to have an obligation to the government. The result is slavery. It becomes very clear the relationship that the people have with the government is slavery, a relationship by violent compulsion. Of course the government does not resort to violence right away. First there is a request and a demand based on fraud, and if that does not work then the government resorts to direct extreme violence. The relationship the people or citizens have with the government is touted as and supposed to be one of voluntary compliance, in other words a voluntary contract/agreement between each other. As we begin to see the details of how government operates, it becomes unbelievably true that the government is based on and operates on a big lie. What is more scary is that the government again and again declares and proclaims that it has no obligation to protect the people but constantly demands through threats of violence that the citizen must pay taxes to sustain such protection services that the government can deny at will. Basically the government is in a state of corruption and in a position of a tyrant. The biggest reason this continues in America today is the people's lack of knowledge concerning what the law really says in this country. Here and there, the government does get sued and looses and pays out money to people. This is nothing but a tactical move in the Art of War performed on society. The results are blasted all over the television screens in America to keep the deceit and fraud going in the minds of the people. When people see this on television in the back of their mind they keep believing people have some kind of rights respected by the government and that government can be held accountable for certain actions. In the mean time one thousand people are denied their rights while one case is granted in the favor of the people. Judges that make these rulings are well aware the strategies of war that are employed in the control of the people. After all, these judges that control the courts and make the rulings are supposed to be highly educated men and woman that know the laws of this country very well. So somewhere along the path of their education and raise to position of judge they have to of figured out the truth of what is going on and what has been going on since the beginning of the United States Corporation posing as government. Some attorney's might be able to claim that they are unaware of the corruption and true nature of the government, if they are idiots that did not pay attention in

Law school. For the attorney's that have risen to the position of a judge there is no excuse. Especially to the position of judge on a Federal level. All these judges on a State and Federal level have basically decided to participate in the corruption and criminal activity of the government. Not only becoming willing accomplices in the crimes but very active participants performing important roles in the perpetuation of this treason against the people. All these judges profit very handsomely and live very rich, like self appointed gods over the people. For example a retired Federal judge was quoted in a San Bernardino newspaper in 2012 about a medical marijuana case concerning state rights, retired Federal judge Larson was quoted as saying:

"... If you take an overview of the history of the U.S. since the founding constitution, a general erosion of state rights and growth of Federal power, that's been the general trend for 225 plus years.."

The retired judge clearly knows what is going on. In this case the states rights that he is referring to is laws voted into existence by the people of the state of California. This retired judge speaks as if he never participated in such behavior. As a Federal judge at one point and time in his career he has to have aided and abetted the erosion of people's rights. When a law is voted into power by the people of the country and the state or federal government circumvents the peoples will and does not respect the people's law, the judges are guilty of treason. They have overstepped their bounds and their only legitimate purpose to exist. Any other explanation is just a bunch a lies. There is no explanation available because the people in government are there to follow and due the peoples will. The government cannot say they don't like the people's choice of law to implement. It does not work that way in this country. Better explained, it's not supposed to work like that in this state or this country. Well, that is what the government is portrayed as. It is claimed by politicians to be a government of "We the people", where all the power comes from the people and the government is just the mechanism through which it is expressed. There are many court rulings that clearly state this principle and in California it is in the California Constitution in Article 2 Section 1 which says:

"All political power is inherent in the people."

Nowhere does it say that government is superior to the people. Although that is how judges, politicians, and government employees behave on an everyday basis. There is so many it will make you dizzy. For the attorneys that went to law school that would say law is too complicated for the average American to understand, I say " the scam is up, give it up". Back in the "Declaration of Independence" there is a part that reads:

> *"… Governments are instituted among men, deriving their just powers from the consent of the governed."*

I quote this not as true wisdom, because the Founding Fathers who wrote this were liars and two-face cheats, but to show that this was promoted to the people because this is the only powers government could possibly exercise that the people would accept as just. Powers that would be granted to governments through consent of the governed. Consent is not true consent when extorted through violence from someone or through the threat of violence.

Now there is something even more interesting about Citizenship. What if someone does not want to be a citizen? What if someone wants to be left alone and does not want any services from the society or government? What if someone wants to live on this so called "Land of the Free" on some mountain without help or service of the government and live off the land? Where does the government justify property taxes or implementation of regulation on someone's land. Here again wee see the scam of government for what it is. Nothing but slavery in disguise. In the Ballentines Law Dictionary we see the following definition of slave:

"A person owned by and bound to another..."

I don't like drugs but if the neighbor wants to do them or kill himself smoking tobacco or drinking gasoline for breakfast, who am I to tell him no or force him by violence or incarceration to stop. Better yet who is the government to say someone can't do such things to themselves. Government puts people in cages for years for using drugs. It at the same time decides you can smoke tobacco and kill yourself if you like, but not cocaine, marijuana, or heroin. Oh, and no hallucinating on poisonous mushrooms either. Although in the event you want to drink alcohol its ok. When people are put in cages and chained like dangerous animals for simply altering their mind with unapproved substances, that is a form of slavery. It is as if a person is owned and bound to another, the legal definition of slavery, not the "Land of the Free". Now, I know that this might sound a little extreme at first. Maybe and most likely because of the years of mental conditioning people have been exposed to in America. This is the "Land of the Free" right? The California Constitution does recognize that "all people are by nature Free and Independent...", right? This in Article 1 Section 1 of the

California Constitution. So how is someone forcefully bound to a society, to a government or to a vote of another? The legal definition in Ballentines Law Dictionary of the word "Free" is :

"Without restraint or coercion, not enslaved; not bound;..."

So how is someone rightfully restrained from doing drugs or eating a mushroom that will make you hallucinate? How can government coerce people to join their political society? When government imposes rules on someone without consent, and the individual is not violating anyone's rights, how does it justify this? If people in America are "Free" then how can an American be punished for selling raw milk from a cow to a ready and willing voluntary buyer? The nature of this "Land of the Free" becomes exposed for what it really is... a modern day slave plantation. Is it voluntary to be compelled by violence or threats of violence to join a society? Ballentines Law Dictionary defines "Voluntary" as:

"Intended. Not by compulsion or accident."

There are many people that would gladly not want to be part of the political society in America. There are many valid reasons why. The United States government drops bombs and kills innocent women, men, and children all over the world. This happens when the United States corporation known as government decides it is in the best interest of the country to start a war and kill a bunch of people that they decide are not worthy to live. These decisions are made without the peoples consent. As recent as the war in Iraq, was even started without even consent from the Congress themselves. That war was started by declaration of the decision of one man - George Bush. Even the other warmongers in Congress' part of the government did not like that.

As we see all the protesters on T.V. protesting wars, obliviously some people do not agree. Then when the government steals from other countries, the people do not get a cut of this robbery, but only a bill for the expense of funding the robbery of any particular nation. The bill is sent to the people in the form of taxes.

Currently there is no option to participate in society or not. People are forced to accept the rules, laws created by the government. There is no choice. People are forced by violent compulsion. Many people are just participating by accident, but not because they intend to. Simply try and

NOT be a citizen and you will quickly discover that there is no option. Police officers and enforcement agents of all types will laugh at you and think you are crazy if you ever tell them that you can for example buy and sell raw cow milk between you and five good neighbors. You will get a citation and have to deal with it in court. You will have to explain to a man in a black suspicious looking robe why you think you can do that. Tell the man that calls himself "judge" and you will discover you are a slave to him by his response. If you would like to buy raw cow milk, why would you have to explain yourself to a stranger? He will tell you it is the "Law", you must follow it. The "Law" is nothing more than the will of another man or group of men, and you are bound to these other men's ideals. Therefore you are not free, you are their slave. Point blank. From experience I know the government in America does not respect free men or people that don't want to participate in government. In the year 2001 I personally sent notice to many government agencies letting them know that I chose to give up my U.S. Citizenship. I notified the government entities that under the Expatriation Act of 1868 anyone can give up their citizenship to the U.S. This congressional act clearly states that no government agent can question or deny someone's choice to expatriate, or in other words to give up their U.S. Citizenship status. The Act clearly says that any government questioning anyone why they wish to give up their citizenship does not represent the U.S. government because preventing someone from giving up their citizenship goes against the very principles this government was founded on. Regardless, the government people working at the U.S. Justice Department decided to send a letter to my home telling me that I could not give up the U.S. Citizenship while staying on this land. The letter said I would be declared a "Pirate" by law and that I could be incarcerated "indefinitely" for failure to have citizenship to any country. It further stated that I was a citizen according to them. Anyone can try this themselves and see what response you will get. I really do not advice it though, but merely tell of my experience in experimenting with freedom. The government never sent anyone to my home to arrest or detain or speak to me, and I have not heard anything about the matter since. According to the courts I am still under their jurisdiction or subject to their control as a slave, as I have been treated as such in afterward interactions with the government. So much for being free.

Chapter 8

Conflict of Interest

The biggest problem to obtaining true free and independent status as the California Constitution claims people have is the major conflict of interest in the government. There is a conflict of interest in the highest degree within government because of the corporate nature of the government, and based on the fact that without people to govern and control, government employees would have no one to regulate and extract money from to pay their salaries. Therefore government representatives such as prosecutors and judges refuse to willingly without resistance follow the rule of law. Even if it is the law they claim is valid and binding on all people, for example the Expatriation Act of 1868 or to uphold and support the California Constitution. The laws are only valid when it serves the interest of furthering and expanding government control over the people they claim to serve. Really judges, police, and prosecutors serve themselves and not the people in the community. Many if not all government agencies are structurally designed to give a bigger paycheck to the employees when there is more "business" to conduct. This business could be more traffic tickets, more criminal cases, more parking violations, more city ordinances to enforce, more child support to extract, more business licenses to sell or any other "business" the government has to interact with peoples lives. That is why every year more laws and regulations come into existence. Interestingly many laws are created and initiated by government are called "bills" as they are going through the approval process to become laws. Basically that is what a law is, a "bill" to the people to extract money in some sneaky and insidious indirect way. This is how the government is known to raise money when they need it. If we look at the countries 225 year history, there is not one year when the government doesn't claim to need more money than the last year. Coincidence, not really. Is it a conspiracy to take the peoples property? Maybe, or it could just be the design of the government allows and encourages this type of unchecked growth. It could just be the human nature in a capitalistic society. One thing is for sure is it has been going on since the beginning of government and the national debt is getting bigger every year with no end in sight. Even worse is that by design the government is destined to implode as evident by cities and counties like San Bernardino in

California filing for bankruptcy. This county admitted in the newspaper to spending 75 percent of the cities general fund on the yearly fire and police agencies in 2012. Every year politicians running the local government raise their salary and the salary of the fire and police departments in exchange for the votes of the fire and police unions. In this process the people of the community are put last in their needs. The lack of checks and balances and the lack of accountability in local, state, and federal government breeds continued abuse and corruption of the power held by individual agents in all levels of government.

In 2012 in the wake of the investigation of what caused San Bernardino to file for bankruptcy, one politician said that from researching and auditing the last 15 years of documents, 13 years of reported budget reports were said to be fraudulently manufactured. So for 13 years no one noticed or cared to say anything. This is where the conflict of interest becomes evident, there is a code of silence within government that is taboo to expose any wrongdoing or corruption. Maybe because most politicians are involved in some kind of questionable activities themselves. The result is the crumbling of ethics and morals in government which ultimately reduces the quality of life for non-politicians in the community.

The criminal and traffic courts are no exception to the conflict of interest that exist within the design of government structure. The salary of the judges, clerks, and prosecutors depends on the amount of "business" the courts transacts. The "business" the courts transact consist of traffic and criminal convictions that impose fines on people to extract money from them. Some of this money goes directly to the judges Individual Retirement Account. If this is not a conflict of interest that creates a bias judge, then nothing is. So when people of the community are convicted on the slightest charge or evidence, they should not be surprised. Logically the judge is inclined to rule on cases in a manner that brings in the bigger paycheck for him and his family. You can call it corruption or you can call it human nature- but the outcome is a conflict of interest. Without any agency or group of people to oversee government functions, there will never cease to be corruption. The checks and balances that are in place now are inadequate as evident by the health of government and the sorry state of quality of life in America. Most people would say that overall America is doing pretty good. Really America is not doing nearly as good as it could be with the present technology and intellectual potential in America. The only reason most think America is doing pretty good is because the government manipulates the information released through media like television, and newspapers. That is why independent news outlets like www.infowars.com and many other Internet and non-government sponsored information outlets, paint an entirely different picture of what is going on in America.

Conflict of interest exists even in the local police and fire departments. Years ago a high ranking fire official, might have been a captain or chief in California was convicted of setting fires in mountain areas in order to obtain more overtime hours and a bigger salary during fire season. He was taken to trial and convicted of murder, as many people died in the fires he was accused of starting. He set fires to get more hazardous pay, basically to create more "work" or "business" at the expense of the community. All for more money to end up in his pocket. Money is a very tempting motivator.

In police departments the motive is the same - money. Corruption scandals have erupted all over the nation, from big cities to small towns, the corruption has permeated all government. The "Rampart" scandal of the Los Angeles Police Department is one of the many outrageous and unbelievable scandals that have plagued police departments. In order to get more money flowing into police departments there must be justification, such as more crime that needs to be suppressed. Even if that crime is being encouraged, created, and fueled by the police or government agents themselves. The

"Rampart Scandal" was so interesting it seemed like a movie. Police officer Raphael Perez was stealing bricks of cocaine from evidence locker rooms and selling it back to the gangs in the streets they took it from. Transcripts from Raphael Perez' testimony when he turned informant on his own partners, reveals that the corruption was encouraged and condoned from the top ranks of the police department. As a matter of fact the action packed movie in theatres called "Training Day" was based on the "Rampart Scandal" and police corruption in Los Angeles. Money entices corruption, then the lack of checks and balances by non-government agents allows it to happen and flourish until it explodes out of the shadows of government secrecy into the public light. Like the Iran-Contra Scandal where the C.I.A was bringing in tons of cocaine into the inner cities of Los Angeles, the government never stopped the misbehavior. It took a journalist to uncover the bad deeds of the government. Then it all unraveled and a high ranking military agent confessed in front of congress that the military of the United States distributed tons of cocaine into the American streets to raise money for black operations. At the end of this activity - if it ever has ended, resulted in many American families destroyed, many people killed in drug turf wars, and many kids left without parents as they were taken to prison for distributing and using this government provided cocaine. All because there is a huge conflict of interest within government. More crimes equal more work for police, sheriffs, and ancillary services like probation and parole agents. All without any non-government agencies to oversee these police activities to prevent corruption.

One of the most blatantly brazen conflicts of interest that was exposed within the last decade was the scandal called "Cash for Kids" that put hundreds of kids in jail and resulted in the death of at least one kid that committed suicide in custody. In this scandal a local judge was incarcerating kids for the most minor offenses in exchange for monetary bribes from the owner of the local detention center the judge was sending kids too. The judge was busted accepting 2 million dollars in cash for exchange in sending kids to jail. How awful is that? This is why it is a conflict of interest for judges and prosecutors to get a higher or lower paycheck based on the amount of people they convict and put in jail. A simple "google" search on the internet on "government corruption" brings up thousands of incidents reported nationwide. Those thousands of incidents have wrongly denied equal protection of the laws to people. These incidents have ruined many lives and families. Those incidents have also created billions of dollars in revenue for government agents, all at the expense of peoples well being. All due to the conflict of interest when the government policies itself. Books like "Prison Profiteers" expose those that make a living of off this corruption.

Chapter 9

Traffic Tickets

Traffic tickets in traffic court in California are a very interesting subject. I can share some revealing experiences about courts in California. The traffic courts in other states operate in almost the concept of fraud, threats, and violence. In California a traffic ticket is issued to people in the streets for many traffic violations. From some research and investigation I did it appears the tickets are based on the rules of contract. When anyone gets a citation issued in California for any reason by a police officer or deputy sheriff, a signature is always required. When the officer asks the person getting the ticket to sign for it, the officer uses threats to get the person to sign. I once asked an officer what would happen if I do not sign the ticket. The officer said "I would have to take you to jail". Basically he threatened me, and so I signed to avoid the trip to jail in handcuffs. People are asked to sign these tickets in a box at the lower portion of the ticket that states something like this:

"Without admitting guilt, I promise to appear…"

So basically by signing this ticket a person is promising to appear at some traffic court location. So one day I read the rules of contract when I got a ticket for something I wasn't guilty of. According to this ticket by signing I promised to show up at court, and if I did not show up then the court had a right to issue a bench warrant because I broke my "promise to appear". After I read a book on contracts called "Contracts, Examples, and Explanations" by Brian A. Blum, I learned that forcing someone to sign something by using threats or violence makes the contract or promise invalid. So when I got a traffic ticket I signed it and the very next day I sent a notice to the court where I was supposed to appear letting the clerk of the court know that I declare the citation and signature on it void because the police officer threatened to take me to jail if I did not sign the traffic citation. I included the citation number, the date, a brief statement declaring it void because of threats to sign, and I signed it at the bottom. I wanted to see if the court would follow the rules of contracts, since it appeared the rule of contracts where the rules the courts used to legally bind someone to show up for court. I had sent the notice to the "clerk of the court", through the United States Postal Service, with certified mail sticker and with return receipt request that requires a signature from the recipient to accept the mail piece. Then on the day I was scheduled for court, I showed up to court to see what would happen. To my amazement the judge called my ticket case and told me the ticket was dismissed without any explanation. I am not sure why as I asked and the judge told me that I must leave the building. So maybe the judge did follow the rules of contract, and just dismissed the ticket, but it's hard to say for sure. At the same time I had a traffic ticket that I had went to court for and pled not guilty. I requested trial for the ticket. The judge sent me to the clerks office to get my "trial date" after I plead not guilty. At the clerks window I told the clerk I was there for a "trial date". The clerk said I had to pay "bail" to get a "trial date". I told the clerk I would not pay, so the clerk told me I had to go to a bail hearing to see if the judge would "waive" the bail. Five days later I went to a court date for a bail hearing, the judge called my name and immediately stated that she was granting a "bail waiver" since I had appeared and that was enough to prove I would show up for trial. The judge then instructed me to go see the clerk for my trial date. This is where it got interesting. The clerk asked me to put my name and address on a document, then the clerk took it back and wrote a lot of things on it. The interesting part is that the clerk wrote on it that I agreed to pay "$2,500 two weeks before court trial". The clerk also put the court date I had to return on the traffic citation. The clerk then handed me the paper, which was a document with the ability to make two copies onto two other sheets that were attached to the back of it. The clerk handed it back to me and told me "sign this paper" to get your trial date. So I blindly signed the paper without reading it and the clerk quickly took it from my hands and gave me one of the triplicate copies of the paper I signed. I read it at that point and asked the clerk why she wrote "$2,500 two weeks before court trial" on the paper. The clerk said the judge required that payment of $2,500 before the scheduled court trial or the judge would put a warrant out for my arrest.

At that point I was outraged that I would have to pay for a violation that I had not been proved guilty of. I went home and analyzed this document I signed. On this form I had signed, I noticed a section that said "I agree to all the terms and conditions on this form". Basically I had been tricked into signing this form where I "agreed" to what the clerk hand wrote onto the document. So I looked in the contract rules book and in the California Civil Code book where the rules of contract are. The rules say a signature on an agreement/contract can be canceled if it was signed by mistake, or if there was fraud in the inducement of the contract and a few other reasons. So I decided to cancel the "agreement" as it seemed that I had "agreed" on that form to pay the court $2,500 before court, and this gave the judge the power to put the warrant out for my arrest if I did not pay as I "agreed" too by signing this form. So I put a brief statement on a piece of paper with the word "NOTICE" on top, the date, my signature, the citation number and I identified the agreement form by specifying what date I signed the form. I sent it to the court at attention of the "Clerk of Court" stating that I made a "mistake" by signing the agreement and that I declared it void as I was canceling my signature. I sent this notice within 72 hours of signing the form. I sent it through the United States Postal Service certified mail and return receipt requested. Once again to my amazement when I went to court on my scheduled trial date, the judge called my name and told me the case was dismissed without any explanation. When I asked why the judge simply told me to leave the courthouse because I had "no further business" there. I never received a response from the court about my notice. I never paid the $2,500 before the scheduled court trial, or at any time. The judge never put a warrant out for my arrest either. Therefore, I came to the conclusion that the court must have dismissed the tickets based on the fact that I sent the Notice of Cancellation of signature due to "mistake" in the case of signing the agreement/contract to pay $2,500 before court.

In the other ticket when I sent in the "Notice of Cancellation" of the signature, I declared it void or no good because the police officer got my signature on the ticket, where I promised to appear at court, based on a threat that if I did not sign the ticket I would be immediately arrested and taken to jail. In that ticket I sent the notice to the clerk of the court the very next day, and on the day I was scheduled to go to court for it I never had to plead guilty or not guilty because the judge told me it was dismissed without asking me anything except what was my name.

The conclusion I came to after researching tickets and how they operate in the legal world of the courts, is the whole traffic court is operating an extortion scheme on the people of California that are unlearned in law. Since California courts are operating in this manner it is most likely that other states of the union in America operate in a similar concept. The whole system is based on fraud, deceit, lies and just plain trickery. Dishonest government agents taking from people without full disclosure of the true nature and cause of people getting their money taken by judges at court. The staff that work at courthouses can claim ignorance of the fraud being perpetuated on the people on a daily basis, but the judges and clerks of the court are directly aware of the fraud. The judges and their clerks are implicated to the point of no return. The attorneys are just as guilty of aiding and abetting the criminal activity at the traffic courts. There is not one attorney that I have questioned about this fraud that will admit it is a fraud.

Either the attorney's are in denial of the fraud or they are just that severely incompetent. The most disturbing fact is that it appears these attorney's really are incompetent in law regardless of how prestige's the law school they went to. It seems these attorney's went to law school and learned the points of law taught at school in order to pass the class and be able to pass the bar exam in order to get a job as an attorney. Then these attorney's kept learning the "suggested" curriculum to stay informed, but have never deviated from the "suggested" teachings from laws schools or societies they belong to, such as the BAR association that all attorney's must belong to and pay dues to in order to be allowed to practice law in this country.

Law schools in this country teach a very limited aspect of law and procedure to its students, compared to the amount of legal procedure and legal tools that are actually available according to law. That's why after years and decades of very few and specific legal tools and procedures utilized by attorney's in courts, the court system and legal community as a collective entity has by custom lowered the standard of competence for the majority of attorney's. Also the courts have become adept and are used to only very limited procedures employed by attorney's and therefore judges are only comfortable with such commonly used procedures, and other legally available procedures provided for in law are frowned upon by judges.

The result is an unspoken policy that only some legal procedures are accepted and anything else will endanger the attorney's rapport with the judge and the district attorney. Something that is very important if the attorney wishes to have a successful career as an attorney. In the process of all this incompetence throughout the history of the American BAR Association, there has been a steady decline in the intellectual sharpness and requirements to successfully practice law in this country. All to the financial gain of attorney's that can perform inferiorly and still earn a good living and to the prejudice and detriment of the people and country.

Through research and investigation I found certain interesting things about traffic tickets and citations in general that require a signature in the process of being issued. The following is a small piece of the investigation but is very telling in nature.

When I had received a ticket for running a red light, I took the ticket and analyzed everything about the document, I read on the internet chatrooms, I read definitions in the law library, I read cases that challenge the constitutionality of tickets, and read up on every vehicle code quoted on the ticket to discover the source of the power of the government agent to issue this ticket. Out of the few different California Vehicle Codes that were quoted on the ticket, all of them kept referring to California Vehicle Code

Section 40510.5(a)(4) as the implied source of authority for the charging of money as a penalty for the ticket. From the face of the ticket it was possible to learn that the ticket was an agreement or contract in nature by the fact a signature was required. Then this vehicle code section 40510.5(a)(4) spoke of a "written agreement" that must "exist" in order for the clerk of the court to "accept payment" of the bail amount of the alleged violation or infraction. Throughout the entire research and investigation there kept coming up this impression and suggestion that the person being charged money was doing so out of entirely voluntary compliance, which we all know is absurd. The whole traffic ticket process feels compulsory not voluntary as the law kept implying and suggesting. Like when I told the clerk of the court "What if I don't sign the paper to get a trial date?" The clerk said "then you don't get a trial date". That document is one that said I would agree to pay a fine. This must have been the "agreement with the court" the vehicle code 40510.5(a)(4) states must "exist" in order for the clerk to "accept" payment from someone. So maybe when I canceled the agreement through a "Notice", the court could not "accept" or more clearly "take" or "charge" me any money. Whatever the reason, most people would say they would never volunteer to pay any money to the court. The only reason people sign tickets is because they feel they have too. Others sign because when you ask the officer if you have to, the officer will say "yes" or they have to take you to jail. So people sign because of the implied threat of being taken to jail. What people don't know is that a signature cannot be required from someone through a threat. Although the court system in general do operate on this method of extracting signatures through an indirect or direct threat. Of course they must because not very many people would voluntarily sign a paper to punish themselves in any way, through money penalties or otherwise. Trickery is the most effectively widespread means of slavery in this country. If the tricks and threats don't obtain voluntary compliance from the people, then the government simply uses violence to force people to comply with the rules they call laws. Subtle extortion is the preferred mode of forcing compliance in order to maintain the appearance of legitimacy and preventing an uprising from society as a whole.

If the secret that all traffic tickets and citations can be avoided by simply learning the rules of contract and sending a notice to the court where they are supposed to appear, the courts would fall apart. Day in and day out thousands of people are extorted for money through these fraudulent transactions. People pay bail to take their ticket to trial because they think they must. Really all they have to do is request a bail hearing and the judge will waive the bail requirements just based on showing up.

To sum it all up, the traffic court scheme is nothing more than a racket and extortion operation that functions smoothly because of societies lack of knowledge. Point blank. Once again, if you ask an attorney if the rules of contract apply, he might tell you they don't. With no reason why they don't, when by legal definition the tickets appear to be contracts. Attorney's not only claim ignorance to any speak of such opposition to complying blindly to government demands, they frown upon anyone who even mentions the concept of questioning authority. Most people who question authority of government are considered crazy or conspiracy theorist and relegated to the class of unimportant opinion holders but as you will see in your own research concerning these traffic tickets and other aspects of government operations, there is some type of dishonest activity behind the basic function of government. Shocking as it may sound, by the definition for the word "conspiracy", in regular English dictionaries or in Law dictionaries that define a word legally, the government activities could be seen as a conspiracy. Most people that claim otherwise do not have knowledge of their own personal investigation concerning such topics to speak in a relevant light. Even when it is a professor of law or a law enforcement officer or anyone that we would expect to be highly informed. There is a common trend amongst people to mindlessly believe these so called experts without knowing where these people's information come from. You would think all government officials would know what they are talking. Let's look at the title of a sheriff or police officer. These agents have the title of "Law Enforcement Officer", but they are not trained in law. The officers are given a 6 month training on how to jump fences and how to properly fill out paperwork to process someone into jail. Nonetheless, people will believe a police officer about what the law says. Ask a police officer if he ever studied the rules of contract and they will tell you no. Yet they issue tickets to people and ask you to sign a contract when asking you to sign a ticket. I really believe that intentionally hiring incompetent people to enforce something they know nothing about is vital to keep people in the current state of bondage and slavery. It cannot possible be an accident to hire people that lack the knowledge about the field they work in, not in today's advanced technological society. Police officers of course would be insulted to hear they are ignorant of how the law operates because they are "Law Enforcement Officers", some maybe have been doing this for 10 or 20 years. What an astonishing fact that these individuals have never bothered in all their years to learn exactly what it is they enforce. Even attorneys that do study for years, for some odd reason don't step outside the confines of accepted practice to learn the law and it's procedures completely. The most obvious reason is because there is no monetary incentive to learn, and most likely fear to find out the truth of their profession, that is if they have not already found out. In society nowadays there is heavy pressure to conform to the status quo, whatever it might be. If you are talking about illegal gangs, elementary kids, or grown up professionals in government such as police officers, councilmen, or judges and attorneys, they are all people that are subject to social peer pressures that are direct and indirect. Everyone it seems is scared to stir up any dust within their profession, especially in government due to the gang-like and actual criminal conduct within these agencies paired with the desirable financial rewards of such jobs. Therefore the probability that clerks of the court, or internal investigators of these agencies would reveal any wrongdoing are highly unlikely. In instances where wrongdoing is revealed, the whistle blower is ousted, blackballed, and made an example of to prevent others from doing the same.

Chapter 10

Criminal Courts

The criminal courts are no exception to the fraud, deceit and lies that are employed on the people of this country to keep people in the slavery that exist today. This country and government proclaims it is the "land of the free and home of the brave", but as we see it for what it is, this country is full of mostly the opposite. True freedom to live and direct ones life is long gone if it ever existed. Brave people also are rarity since new rules and laws are created every year to quickly remove them from society. Simply defending yourself in a situation can result in landing in jail. In self defense situations many have seriously hurt the assailant and have become criminals themselves. Government is constantly and steadily making people more dependent on it for protection that it is not obligated to provide.

Although I would be heavily inclined to cite many laws, cases as examples, and studies and reports to illustrate the American trend into deeper slavery, or the existence of slavery today, I will refrain. There are tons of such documentary material to do just that but I feel it will make people lose a sense of reality of the situation with overwhelming volumes of such data. Common conversational dialogue I believe is more effective in demonstrating the problem of modern day slavery in America today. First of all America is one of the, or the country with more people per capita in jail or prison than any other nation on earth. The land of the free puts more people in jail for the most common and petty offenses than any other in the world! Heck, in America there is even a federal law that can land anyone in federal prison for owing more than ten thousand dollars in child support debt. Everyone should pay any legitimate debt they owe, but to imprison someone for years for owing an amount as little as ten thousand dollars is ridiculous. Just like the debtors prisons of England, we have it here in

America today.

There is actually laws on the books that say people cannot be put in prison behind debt owed, but it happens everyday in America.

Another obvious tactic of manipulation the criminal court system employs on people that reveals the nature of the court is bail. People charged with crimes are most always jailed until the close of trial to see if they are innocent or guilty. First off people are deprived of freedom while waiting to go to trial to determine guilt. While waiting for trial people are allowed to bail out of jail and fight their case from the outside of jail, if they can post bail. Posting bail is nothing more than paying a certain amount of money for this option to fight the charges from outside of jail. So, if a person does not have the money to pay bail they have to stay in jail deprived of freedom, even though the courts have not deemed someone guilty. If you can pay you can get out of jail on bail, if you can't, you don't.

This is not "justice for all." Just another lie on the slave plantation called America. While people wait for trial in jail they are subject to lack of sleep, lack of proper food, starvation and exposed to the violence of jail. Not only are people in jail exposed to daily violent situations in between inmates, worst of all people are exposed to extremely violent deputies that run the jails and are worse than the inmates. Many deputies have obvious mental problems as they are known to assault and murder inmates for the most trivial issue. Not only have I personally witnessed such activities in county jail it has made it to the news. In 2011 or 2012 it was reported in the Los Angeles Times Newspaper that the FBI had sent undercover Federal agents into Los Angeles County Jail to investigate the numerous mysterious deaths happening in the jail. The story of corruption and violent culture in the L.A. County Jail reads like a movie script and not in a good way, but in a cruel and gruesome story of what inmates there are subject to in the form of officer brutality. After an investigation by Federal agents undercover posing as inmates brought to national headlines the blatant violations of the law by the sheriff deputies that run the jail. The scariest part is that the entire sheriff's department was implicated up to the sheriff and the sheriff himself. People were killed violently by the deputies on a regular basis for over a decade before anything was done to address the issue. In the meantime people suffered every day in these places awaiting trial and a speedy trial being nowhere within reach for most. The outcome is that many plead guilty just to get out of jail or to get transferred to a prison where conditions are mysteriously more humane. What a shame that people that are not convicted are exposed to inhumane and violent starving conditions and once an inmate is convicted he is granted a more peaceful setting where he is given more food and better sleeping conditions. A coincidence, I think not. The outcome is very predictable when you starve, beat, and prevent from adequately sleeping or providing themselves a meaningful defense in court. Anyone is going to want to plead guilty just to remove themselves from those cruel and horrible conditions, even if it means the condition just getting marginally better such as receiving a little bit more food.

Unfortunately these conditions have existed and do exist in jails and prisons today. How just is that? All the while prosecutors and judges brag about how people have been afforded a fair and just process. The court system is so corrupt and knows It operates on violence and duress, threats, and menace to obtain guilty pleas out of people, that when people sign guilty pleas in court, the judge forces the person to say that no threats, duress, undue influence, or menace was used by the court, judge or prosecutor to obtain a guilty plea. People are forced because if you don't plead guilty then people are returned to jail to continue to suffer the starvation and violence dished out by deputies. In San Bernardino County there is a standard template form used in all guilty pleas accepted by the court. Section 12 of this form that is an agreement to plead guilty says that the person/inmate signing the form agrees no threat, menace, duress, or undue influence of any kind was used to get them to plead guilty. The reason that is there is to cover the crime that those exact methods were employed to get the person to sign. Threats, menace, duress, and undue influence render any agreement void according to well established and recognized rules of contract.

This method amounts to extortion, fraud and plain old slavery by the definition of the law. In California and America slavery and such behavior is prohibited by law. Or so we thought. There is public and widely known statistics that many people are wrongly accused and convicted in this country every day. How can this be? Very simple when we consider the for profit nature of the court system coupled with absurd laws on the books, anyone nowadays can call the police and say they were threatened by someone and that "someone" is going to jail or to be more exact the torture facility. All with no evidence whatsoever except someone's word. To make it worse a threat is a felony in California. Therefore no more owning a gun, can't go hunting. No more getting many well-paying jobs, sometimes you can't even visit certain countries with a felony. Now you must stay on the Slave Plantation in America. Slavery has always been a popular method of organizing society throughout history. In this day and age in America the court system is nothing more than a slightly modified version of ancient European Slavery where people belonged to separate classes such as nobles, the common people and other crafty labels of control and segregation. Most of these labels are nothing more than tools of discrimination to divide and conquer the slaves of the kingdom.

In the criminal court system of America there is an option called a "petition for writ of habeas corpus", this petition is a process by which a wrongly imprisoned person can petition or more accurately "beg" the higher courts to review the imprisonment of someone. The whole process first of all is based on the old process of begging the king for something. The title "writ" as defined in law dictionaries means the order, command or decree from a king. In America the King or owner of the slave plantation has set up a group of men and women that have the title of judges to deal with the begging slaves. Once again the King hides his face by hiring people to do his dirty work. These judges gladly follow the laws and rules on the books unless someone gets too close to the truth that exposes the slavery or if you question the slavery in America itself. Honestly, what else can the people expect from men that feel and behave as self-appointed gods. These judges are virtually exempt from the laws of the country. That is why these judges are so loyal to the King running the slave plantation; there whole life substance is financially dependent on the undisclosed amounts of money and gifts that they receive.

It is my observation that these judges have been mentally conditioned through years of exposure to such behavior of exemption from the laws through corruption, that they are hard pressed to see the reality of their insanity. Judges are often drunk with the power they wield and enforce through law enforcement officers that do the dirty work of effecting violence on people for such things is simply failing to provide a name. Is this mere speculation? No. In a criminal case I was physically beat and assaulted by Sheriff Deputy Roosevelt Dutra from the Victorville Sheriff's department for failure to provide a name even though my fingerprints revealed who I am through DMV records. To make the government's agent's insanity and mental illness even clearer, the deputy took me to a hospital called St. Mary's Hospital in Apple Valley California where I was threatened with "insane" if I did not agree I was this name the deputy demanded. According to the deputies police report it was the Sheriff's department policy to take someone to a hospital and physically assault them and declare them insane and inject them with mind altering drugs if anyone failed to answer what their name is. Yes, that simple. So this clearly shows the sick and violent nature of the infirm judges that allow and endorse such policies and behavior. Judges might try to distance themselves from such practices but nonetheless are guiltier than the perpetrators. Sure they have procedures in place to file law suits and prevent or stop such behavior, but the injury would have already been committed even those law suits and procedures are strategically designed to fatigue people into giving up, oh, and of course there is a 350 dollar initial filing fee. That's if you know the law and procedure yourself if not then an attorney will charge 30,000 dollars and up to file it for you. Once again there are deterrents around every corner to prevent successful law suits against government corruption and unnecessary violence. In all fairness I must say, that although uncommon to succeed in a suit against government, it is possible and these successful suits are publicly paraded to the population through media to perpetuate the illusion of freedom and rights in America. These cares are nothing more than strategic military operations against the minds of the uninformed public. A silent war against the minds of the people is in full gear where the weapons are of intellectual instead of forceful nature.

Criminal court proceedings give everyone the option of having a jury trial where the people of the community determine the guilt or innocence of someone. These jury trials are a farce, there is no fairness to them for many reasons. The most significant tool to control the outcome of a jury trial is the fact that the judge determines what evidence the jury can hear. A prospective witness in a case is told to "swear to tell the truth, the whole truth, and nothing but the truth." Then the judge tells him what he can and cannot say on the witness stand during his testimony, another clear contradiction in the court system. This way courts can shape the outcome of the jury through manipulating the information the jury is allowed to hear.

In all criminal cases the accused is told by the judge that he has the right to a speedy trial or he can waive time, then he is asked what he would like to do. In case SA302111 out of Santa Monica Court in department "C", I was told the same. I said I would like a speedy trial and the judge told me I didn't know what I was talking about. So then why does the judge ask the question? Once again to give the appearance of fairness and rights. A complaint to the commission of Judicial Performance that regulates judges behavior determined the Judge did nothing wrong. So obviously he behaved appropriately. There was too much at stake in that case I had been falsely accused of murder and attempted murders simply because I was in the area.

At trial the case quickly fell apart as officers testified that all evidence had been falsified. Even the witnesses called the district attorney a liar at trial in front of the jury. Falsified evidence and no government agent were prosecuted. When I refused to plead guilty at one point, Judge Bernard Kamins in Santa Monica Superior Court clearly told me:

"I send innocent people to prison for the rest of their life all the time."
- *Hon?* Judge Bernard Kamins (Emphasis Added)

That was his response when I told him I was innocent and could not plead guilty, a shocking statement to hear from the face of the government. I still maintained a sense of hope for a while even after the appalling revelation about his character and nature of the court system.

Slavery has been in effect for a long time. Citizenship which is the modern label for slavery is the tool of enslavement. Although someone can give up citizenship, you must claim citizenship from another country. Basically trade slave master or the man will not be left alone. The violent nature of this government is arbitrary in dishing it out. If it feels like it needs to be violent to maintain its power and control, then it will. Kings and

Queens rule the entire world and America is no exception. Kings have just used more sophisticated meant to control the people. Electrical technology is making huge leaps in progress every 6 months all while our concept of government keeps its same draconian posture for centuries. There is only a slight transformation every 50 years or so in the labeling and wording used in the legal system of America. Intellectual word play is one of the main tools of deception, probably the most important and effective.

In court English words have legal meanings that are different than the meaning in the regular English dictionary. Definitions in law are relegated to an entirely different language although they are English words; they speak a totally different language, because the definition in legal language in court means something else. Over the years of development of this government the criminal courts have not evolved in the face concerning procedure or penal nature to correct and rehabilitate people. Laws continuously change but the nature is the same, to incarcerate people and then spit them back into society without any meaningful correction or rehabilitation. Therefore the likelihood of a more peaceful and productive man in society is not increased. Prisons are in the business, yes business, as in for profit of making money off the inmates while incarcerated. Some corporations financially gain so handsomely that from a business profit point of view it is in their best interest for crime to continue in order to have people to incarcerate. Books like "prison profiteers" expose the massive fortune corporations generate through incarcerating people.

The legal system in America only evolves in the advanced methods to manipulate the removal of people's rights. In turn people accused of crimes develop contempt not just for the legal system but for the government in general. This dangerous combination potentially creates more crimes and or discontent in the communities. The outcome is not good for the health of the society as a whole. It slows down progress for the average person and inhibits intellectual levels that in the long run can only create two separate classes of very rich and very poor people, only creating a never ending cycle of stagnation for mankind. The implications are grave in the long run as history will clearly explain. Corruption and lack of accountability in government quickly ruin any good intention in all government.

Chapter 11

Money

All the corruption and greed that creates the slavery of the country would not be possible without the monetary system in America. The current monetary system in America is another powerful tool to enslave people. The money system in America is not run by the American government for the benefit of the American people. The current system is run for the benefit of a handful of wealthy private bankers. The Federal Reserve Bank is a private corporation in the business of printing designs on paper and selling that paper at an extremely high mark up in order to generate astronomical profits for the private individuals that own the Federal Reserve Banking system. It might be a hard truth to swallow at first but it is the truth.

The government hired this private company to print the paper money somewhere around 1933, why would the government do such an unwise move that has put the country in debt? It all depends on what angle you look at. Some say it's a conspiracy to steal the wealth of the people, others might say it was just a bad decision and the government did not foresee the long term undesirable side effects. The reason new is pretty much irrelevant. The only thing that matters now is the fact that the current money system is sinking the people into slavery more and more by the day. The national debt to this private group of bankers is literally in the tens of trillions of dollars and increasing every year in a snowball effect. Some say the system is even intentionally designed to increase the debt every year. For example if the private company called the Federal Reserve Bank lets the U.S. Government borrow 100 pieces of paper called one dollar bills and the U.S. government has to pay back 130 pieces of papers of the same kind, but there is only 100 of those pieces of papers in existence and only the Federal Reserve Bank can print these pieces of paper. How then can the debt be paid back? It literally cannot pay back the debt because the other 30 bills do not exist to be paid back. Even if the government took back all the bills in circulation it would still only have the 100 paper bills it borrowed from the Federal Reserve Bank. So it is obvious that the country can never get out of debt from this private company, but what real effect does this system of debt have on the people of the land? The real effect for the people is prices that are insanely higher on anything they buy, a reduced quality of living for people everywhere. If the people could simply print their own paper bills to conduct trade and commerce, everyone's quality of life would immediately increase. From a logical standpoint of view there is no good reason why the U.S. government would contract out the job of printing paper money to a private company and even worse at an extremely high cost that makes no sense for the country. Either the politicians are that incompetent or they conspired against the people to steal the riches of the nation. The only result for the people is a reduced quality of living, slavery and debt bondage for generations to come and possible civil unrest at some point when the people figure out the fraud is being enforced against them.

After an analysis and close examination of the American monetary system, the conclusion is that there is absolutely no reason for the government to have a monopoly on the issue of the money supply. There is no reason for government to control money at all. In America there are communities that issue private local currency in their communities with very desirable results. It increases trade, buying and selling and encourages the economy to grow which increases the quality of life for all people involved. One such community that has local paper currency is the town of Ithaca in New York. There is also a few others. There was even the "Liberty dollar" that was backed by gold and silver but the company has been shut down. The company owner was prosecuted for making money similar to the U.S. government money, which is a crime on a federal level. The "Liberty dollar" was a nationwide currency that became very successful and popular as it was paper money backed by gold and silver deposits. Money must be controlled by government to properly enslave the people and make people work significantly harder to acquire anything and provide food for their children.

Government is addicted to the power to control the people of this country by using methods that appear well intentioned but have the end goal of control. All methods of government are designed to intrude into important aspects of people's lives and prevent true freedom. There is no legal or honest justification for controlling the money supply of the country. There is only one purpose – Slavery. Many people in the country are convinced that the monetary system in America must be government controlled. Usually those are people that know nothing about the money system in America, its history or how it works. The Federal Reserve regularly announces nation's inflation on the currency in America. Inflation is just a fancy word for intellectual methods of thievery. If we look at what a quarter could buy when it was made out of silver we can see the problem with having a private company regulate money in America, with the intention of turning a profit. A quarter made of fine silver as they were made approximately in the 1950's could today in 2012 buy about two gallons of gas at four dollars each. A silver quarter is worth about eight dollars in paper Federal Reserve notes. A silver quarter can be taken to any jewelry store or pawn shop and convert it into Federal Reserve notes instantly. Now if we look at how much a quarter that is not silver can buy, compared to one that is silver, the difference is ridiculous. A silver quarter can buy 2 gallons of gasoline. A regular 2012 quarter that is not silver can buy about one sixteenth of a gallon of gasoline. The amount of inflation in the last 60 years is insane and at its current rate of inflation will crash the country's economy, all because the fabricated imaginary debt created by the ingenuity of the Federal Reserve Bank Corporation.

Without the Federal Reserve Banking system having the power to print paper money it would not be able to wield so much influence and control over the people in America. Politicians and government agents would not have the power to give away all this money to bribe its way into control of people's lives, without this fraudulent money system. According to the book "Creature from Jekyll Island", a group of politicians and bankers put the Federal Reserve Bank into power by probably guaranteeing riches in this paper money to politicians. A brilliant scheme foisted upon the people of the country. It seems that government is destined to overstep its assigned role in every way possible. Governments throughout history have consistently lived up to a bad name. In America the current status as a modern day slave plantation is not a surprise for history students. Without the people paying attention to history, it really does repeat itself. The temptation to steal and control people must be huge for politicians, as evident by the fact that it is rampant in the American government. The money system in America is closely guarded by big words and a confusing structure, at first the theft of people's livelihood through intellectual trickery.

In December of 2012 the American government is claiming to be facing a "fiscal cliff," Supposedly a financial crisis that will force the raising of taxes on the middle class and the rich, a fabricated status of classes created by the natural side effect of a corrupt and dishonest money system. There are over 400 members of congress that can't seem to come to a solution as to how to balance a yearly budget. Overpaid politicians that are in cahoots with each other to oppress people and use the money system as the means to achieve it. Every year the financial situation of the country gets worse. All these highly educated men and women can't come up with a sound financial plan to get out of debt, but billions of dollars are spent that are unaccounted for all while local teachers are fired for lack of funds. Many parks around the state of California closed for lack of funding, and then an audit found 54 million dollars hidden in an account. Coincidence that there is no one held accountable? Of course not, simple, you scratch my back type corruption. This lack of accountability for crimes is purposely inserted into the modern day slave plantation in order to encourage theft and hinder the people's progress. Government policies of lack accountability are set at the highest realm of government. The present day owners of government that enforce and maintain the slave status of the population have an interest in preventing people's financial progress. Slaves that are kept in a lacking capacity are to busy trying to earn a living and cannot focus on developing their mind and knowledge about much else. Mentally imprisoned slaves on a huge plantation where intellectual advanced methods restrict peoples advancement in knowledge is accomplished through many means. The less obvious the control methods the least likely people will notice.

Some congressmen such as Ron Paul have exposed the corruption of the Federal Reserve Bank. Ron Paul has on several occasions spoken out against the money system, without success. That should be no surprise as the power of the Federal Reserve is beyond amazing. The power to print money allows bribery at the highest levels. At whatever cost it's really going to take many honest and brave people to speak out to release the country from the slavery. President John F. Kennedy is said to have issued an executive order to print interest free money without going through the Federal Reserve Bank. The printing of that interest free money was going to start the day after he was killed for all to see in broad day light. The next day the money never issued, never printed and that executive order was not implemented. What a big coincidence.

Becoming more common, the national debt is spiraling out of control and many other issues are attracting the people's attention. The tax issue is a very important issue to many in the country and when the federal government keeps pushing for higher taxes on every family, rich and poor, the wealthy are more likely to proceed through peaceful means of petition and even though the government has confined petitions to almost meaningless and futile methods, things could change. People can create their own non-government approved committees and demand change through the power of massive numbers. The federal government relies on devious and undisclosed clandestine operations by government agencies to break up and suppress any type of organized peaceful effort on behalf of the people

Chapter 12

Real Estate

To enslave an entire nation it takes a lot of thinking. The slavery imposed on the nation is very well situated. The intellectual chains attached to the hands and feet of the American people are many. The real estate industry is also rigged to enslave the people. The money system combined with fraud and trickery in the real estate market keeps the chains heavily and securely attached to people. The goal of owning a home, ranch, or private land as property is a part of the American Dream. Many if not most working class Americans spent a great portion of their income to secure a piece of private property. If an American buys a home through a loan, it is a loan granted with interest attached to it. The loan must be paid back plus interest with money that has been taxed already at its source. Then at the end of the year the people must pay tax on the property, if it's paid off or not. The entire concept of taxing people's property once it is paid off is ridiculous. The tax money collected from property tax is nothing but extortion money. Services provided by government are funded through a multitude of other taxes. A true accounting of all money collected by government would clearly show a surplus in the hundreds of billions of dollars. It does not take an economist to figure this out. Simply by looking at how much money the Federal government gives away to other countries in the form of financial aid, we know trillions of dollars. Then if we look at the money spent on space travel the picture is clear, the government spends another hundreds of billions a year on just space research alone. All the while local, state, and national governments claim they don't have enough money and must raise property taxes to fund basic services. How preposterous is that? What a joke, really, what a big insult to the people's intelligence. If space travel alone were suspended for one single year it would be enough to beautify and rehabilitate all the run down cities of America and some. That's not including all the hundreds of billions of dollars donated to countries around the world. So local politicians do not raise taxes because they must, they do it to push forward a secret agenda; the enslavement of the American people and the secured enslavement of the people's children. The sad part is that most politicians can't see past what is in front of them, the bigger plan of slavery they are unwitting participants in. Most politicians it seem vote on laws based on what is popular or based on what they have been bribed to vote on. Bribery is now legalized in politics; they are called donations or contributions to campaigns. Either way you look at it the effect is a simple bribery.

Property is a favorite target for politicians to attack, and attack on many different levels through many creative tactics. Even the recent real estate bubble bust of the country was a fabricated fraud, all with the intention of taking people's property. Many national banks and major real estate companies have been accused of committing fraud against people when foreclosing on people's homes. There are many court cases against Chase Bank, Bank of America and other banks accused of committing fraud. Sure it might be the employees that are conducting the activity, but the employee's behavior is condoned and encouraged by bank executives. Even more disturbing, the criminal behavior is taught to employees by the banks higher up executives that set policy for the banks. So really employees are just doing what they are told and paid to do. If they don't do as told the bank fires them and hires someone that will do as told.

The entire real estate mortgage is a scam designed to steal from people and more importantly designed to keep people in slavery by charging people exuberant amounts over the true cost of properties values. When someone buys a home from the bank there is many documents to sign in order to get a loan. These documents are not explained to the buyer in the sense of legal terms, obligations, or legal definitions of what they really are. People sign documents called "notes" which are then deposited into a bank account and the bank is paid in full. The bank doesn't reveal this to buyers. The paper signed called a "note" is then even resold on the stock market to investors in some creative way where the bank gets paid again. At the same time the bank is receiving payments on this so called "loan" from the buyer that got this imaginary loan. This is in no way a complete legal explanation of the process of lending money for home purchases, but merely an oversimplified explanation. Many people are challenging the foreclosure process in court asking to see the original signed "note" that the bank is supposed to have in possession to legally start a foreclosure. The bank instituting foreclosure against someone rarely if ever has the original "note" signed by the buyer. Why? Because the banks by routine and policy sell these "notes" for the face value according to revelations in court documents on such type of cases. By law the bank must return the "note" to the buyer when the loan is paid off, but they can't if they have already sold it. A quick research on the internet brings up many cases where the bank does not have the original note and the court stops the bank from proceeding with the foreclosure. Many people have filed "quiet title" actions in Federal court demanding that the bank produce the original signed note before the bank can proceed with a foreclosure. When the bank does not hold the note, they no longer are entitled to collect on the note. Even if the bank does produce the original note, there is always nondisclosure and fraud involved in the note and or Deed of Trust. Simply study contract law and dissect the documents and the fraud is obvious. The problem now is getting the court to enforce the law. The practice of fraud is so widespread it is literally the industry standard to commit fraud. There are even frauds in the foreclosure process where steps are skipped that are required by law. The show "60 Minutes" did a special on the practices of banks around the country that focused on fraudulent foreclosure practices. A company called Docx LLC was exposed for fraud in signatures required to process a foreclosure. The name of Linda Green was supposedly signed on documents by high school students getting paid to sign thousands of foreclosure documents a day, basically massive fraud. Was anyone prosecuted? Take a guess, probably not anything significant. Banks feel so above the law that it was reported people that never had a loan on their home were getting threats of foreclosure from the banks. How outrageous is that? Banks are to blame for such injustices that are happening and have happened, but the blame is also the people that keep quiet about the fraud. Then there is employees of the bank that participate without the knowledge of the fraud. These people without knowledge are just as guilty because they are in a position to stop it but routinely enforce the fraud through lack of knowledge. Individuals that claim to know the rules, the law, and how things operate and have titles such as "loan officer" insist that they are knowledgeable in the field, all without ever looking up the actual laws or rules. Most bank employees follow what they are taught by the bank they work for; even when they find out they are operating under questionable illegal methods. Employees blindly and mindlessly following marching orders without doing their own research are what have put the nation where it is today. We are all to blame to some extent. Free people can't expect be free very long when they refused to clearly understand what they claim to be experts, specialist, or enforcers of. In the real estate industry the fraud has only been able to flourish because of the arrogance of our so called unmeritorious wisdom, which actually is prevalent throughout many vital fields in America, adding and facilitating the slavery in America.

Chapter 13

Medicine, Food and Education

Slavery in America is so well established because of the control of information by those that set policy in the upper levels of the Federal and State governments. The medicine, food and education sectors of the nation are also avenues through which the slavery is implemented in America. The government in America has openly claimed that it holds back technology for 20 or 30 years from the people in order to protect national security. National security is nothing more than the protection of the current status of slavery in America. The creative labeling of the slavery and related terms is what helps slide the chains over peoples necks, all done openly and easily because of peoples lack of interest to know the truth. Through the public education system the government has set the tone that incompetence is acceptable normal behavior. People stagnate into incompetence through a public education system that limits and restricts people's learning. Children that do not conform to the methods of learning and teaching in American Schools are deemed a problem. These children a lot of the time if not most are labeled inferior and treated as if they are retarded, dumb and are even put on medicine for their alleged mental problems. It's that easy to hold back an entire nation, just simply set the standard of intelligence from some office in Washington D.C. and everyone must follow. Since teachers are paid to do as they are told, they comply or lose their job. Once again the money factor comes into play. The tone is set very low for accomplishments at local schools, while at the same time making education appear complicated enough as if to be actually posing a challenge and providing significant or meaningful learning of valuable information. The elementary schools are even known for having psychologist on the school grounds that deal with these problems or dumb children that refuse to sit still in class. These psychologist offer therapy to kids and included in this therapy are things like prescribing mind altering medication to children as their young minds are still developing. These psychologists are mostly nothing but victims themselves of a broken and inferior schooling system. Yale and Harvard and other prestigious universities are inferior schools along with the rest in the nation. Medication to "Fix" these children s mind are prescribed for children all over the nation with total disregard for the health of children. These psych medications have many side effects that damage vital organs of the body and only show up later in life, where they are so distant in time the pharmaceutical companies are relieved of liability. The Tampering of mental functions is totally unnecessary and irresponsible in 99 percent of the situations. These doctors that prescribe these damaging medications are very well aware of the health risk and the parents should be also since the side effects are public information. Simply asking the prescribing doctor, parent would find out. For some odd reason people are incline to listen to so called "experts" and totally avoid the responsible thing to do and research the risks and benefits of any medication themselves. There is many sources that anyone can look in to learn of the potential side effects of any medication. Even literature distributed by the manufacturer themselves.

The biggest problem in the medical field along with any other field in this country is the lack of individualism. People nowadays behave as the crowds dictate and trickles down to the followers. In many situations this method is very effective to accomplish a common goal and is actually very valuable and desirable. That reality has led many to believe that to question such authority or any structure of authority leaves people vulnerable to those at the helm of the power structure, either through intentional design or through thinking to analyze the results and outcomes of decisions. For the most part information in the current medical field is information that has been filtered and spoon fed to students who become medical professionals who then feed this incomplete information to patients. People are that easily controlled and reduced to slaves who wait for the "experts" to give them information about the medical field. It could be a coincidence that most if not all medicines that doctors prescribe have huge serious side effects of organ damage and possible death. When these dangerous and deadly side effects do strike and maim and kill people, it is seldom if ever reported on the front page of the newspaper or the news on television. Even more ridiculous is that in all but the most simple cases these modern day medications regularly pushed onto people are only to treat the symptoms and not cure the problem. The medicine that does cure a health issue is there basically because after so many decades the information could just no longer be suppressed. One thing for sure is that modern day doctors do not use holistic methods first before resorting to giving someone a pill with numerous side effects. It could be called a conspiracy, or it could be called running a profitable business under a capitalistic model, or just plain greed by doctors that get huge monetary incentives to prescribe a pill instead of using a holistic natural method that is just as effective if not better. Natural medicines are ridiculed and attacked by organizations such as doctors unions even when the natural medicines are hundreds of years old as being effectively documented cures or treatments. At the same time most medicines in a pill form are derived directly from the plants, trees, shrubs, bushes, or other natural sources that government and modern medicine organizations down play. Most of modern day medicine is driven by profit. Doctors participate in the perpetuation of slavery through spreading limited and incomplete information for a financial profit, together with government that outlaws many natural substances of natural origin from plants. This dual control of information keeps people in the dark ages in a modern day future

THC from cannabis plants known as marijuana is a perfect example of this conspiracy. THC in its natural plant form is prohibited by the federal government and effectively banned and removed from hospitals around the nation. The government prohibits natural THC but you can buy the pill form for a ridiculously expensive price from doctors. Even states that allow medical use such as California and another thirteen states have found patients getting arrested and federally charged and jailed for legal behavior under state laws. In 1996 California passed a law allowing use of the plant for medicine, and 16 years later, almost two decades after the law passed, the federal government is still arresting and jailing people regardless of medical necessity and state laws that allow it. The federal government says cannabis has no medical use whatsoever, but the Federal government every month ships hundreds of cannabis cigarettes to federal cannabis patients such as Erv Rosenfield, a stock broker. Also the federal agency that regulates drugs allows the sale and use of THC, the active ingredient in cannabis, to be sold in pill form to patients for medical use. This pill name is called Marinol and is perfectly legal to take with a doctors prescription. On the other hand if anyone uses the equally safe and effective natural version directly from a plant, the government can arrest and jail them.

A man named Aaron Sandusky in January of 2013 was just sentenced to 10 years for running legitimately registered and state approved Medical Marijuana clinics in San Bernardino county. The federal judge in the trial prohibited witnesses and defense from mentioning the fact that Aaron was in compliance with California state law voted in by the voters of the state. So he gets 10 years in a federal prison for doing what the people voted for but the federal government prohibits. The federal government is supposedly a representative of the peoples will, here the truth is revealed who is the master and who is the slave. Americans are proclaimed to be free but a simple and uncomplicated analysis of any aspect of the American government tells the truth. Today's government is the same relationship people have had in the history of kingdoms they think they have escaped. A master and slave relationship where the people are slaves that have no choice but what is approved by the master.

For some reason the government has arbitrarily determined that a natural and safe plant with harmless side effects is not allowed for people to use in its natural plant form. While at the same time selling the synthetic pill version. The federally funded National Institute of Health has even suggested the natural form of the cannabis plant is more effective than the pill version. Even doctors unions in America have verified the safe therapeutic use of natural cannabis. The Food & Drug Administration that approves medicines for doctors to legally prescribe, but at the same time is considering approval of an extract of the natural plant in an oral spray version named SATIVEX. This spray is already available for legal sale in Canada and other developed nations. Since the U.S is considering approval of this spray we must wonder if only Corporate control and distribution is safe and individual peoples choice and decisions are not. In a greatly researched and documented book titled "The Conspiracy against Hemp & Marijuana" by Jack Herer, it is clear that government was used to outlaw this valuable natural plant by wealthy men for the financial gain and profit of certain corporations. Outrageous but true. If it is a conspiracy, intentional or not, the results is the same. The contribution to the systematic and eventual enslavement of the people. Removing choices for people to use natural plant sources for medicine or other use is a key prong to the reduction of people into slaves, and instruments of use for the slave master.

There are many natural plants and herbs that are systematically removed from circulation in America through decree of the slave master king called Laws. Keeping natural alternatives of medicine and food out of peoples reach is another ingenious step to make slaves out of people and keep them there. With government having the ultimate say in so many aspects of people's lives there is no escaping the eventual result of slavery. Many natural plants have nutrients, vitamins and oils that are beyond valuable for optimum health in people. Everyone knows the body requires certain vitamins and nutrition to stay healthy. What people don't generally know is that nutrition can directly influence someone's confidence, self-esteem and other important psychological functions of the mind. The quality of someone's nutrition highly determines people's behavior in life, which in turn literally shapes people's future and quality of life in general. The nutritional intake of people is regulated by the government in America in a very aggressive manner. Government is deeply involved in the tampering of the food supply in the country. Food is even genetically modified by government scientist. Some countries have banned genetically modified foods based on research that it is dangerous to people's health. In America genetically modified foods are sold to people without notice. In the California elections of November 2012 there were propositions that if passed into law would have required foods to be labeled as genetically modified organisms if being sold to the people. One argument would be a tidal wave of lawsuits against such companies. Obviously a tidal wave of lawsuits would only happen if there was justification according to potential or actual side effects from eating such modified foods. So basically these companies said don't pass the law because if the people find out what we are doing to the food and the dangerous health effects, they will sue us in droves. That itself tells how dangerous the food probably is. It's unbelievable that people that work in these companies feel they have no moral obligation to voluntarily put labels on these foods. They know better than anyone else the long term health risk. Our gain has people doing things that will eventually hurt society as a whole. The fact that so many industries in America operate on the same principles of moral deficiency subliminally encourage many to behave the same. Now the restrictions and control of the food supply have brought upon the people many health issues as the inevitable result. America has some of the highest rates of heart disease, diabetes, cancers and even mental health issues in the world. People should know something is not right when such a technology advanced nation has some of the worst quality of health. By the government controlling the food supply, the quality of the food supply and the types of food people can consume, people are deprived of the true benefits of our advanced technological times. Because although there is much interference by government agencies covertly and overtly, there is much independent research done in the private sector and the information is available for the public to find. As a matter of fact the libraries and internet are full of amazing discoveries that good intentioned people make available to anyone looking for it.

It is no mystery then why government is busy keeping the masses entertained and busy with meaningless and mindless activities, such as: watching sports and the funding of distracting activities. Even such activities that are educational in nature are really limited in an informational aspect compared to the true extent of information available on any given subject. Education in America has not really progressed with the informational developments of technology. If anything, government ensures that the intellectual development of the nation is restricted and limited through the exact educational system that is supposed to be informing the nation's population. Just like the farms that are supposed to be producing fruits and vegetables for the nation to consume, are very frequently paid by the government to not produce any food. Government regularly pays large farms to not grow any food and let the land barren for a season or more, all in the name of controlling food prices. These artificially created food shortages are to manipulate and maintain food prices at certain levels. There is no justification for paying farmers to not grow any food on their land.

Education in America is an insult in light of the fact that superior and advanced information is available for the people to learn. In industries of nutrition, health, energy, electronics, math, science and every other subject taught in schools in America there is so much more information that is not taught and is intentionally held back from students. The public education system sets the pace of learning and sets the parameters of what is perceived as advanced knowledge. The end result is what the country is today, a population of slaves that don't know enough world history to realize they are slaves in a modern world, where government funds studies in the hundreds of millions of dollars to learn human behavior and employs in conversational hypnosis in political campaigns and subliminal programming in television and cartoons, and so much more. There is third world countries that are producing a more intellectual and efficient population through their education systems. India is said to have superior scientist, china has smarter kids, South Korean government has a far superior education system and Mexico is even said to have a better education system and a better economy according to recent studies. As a country Americans need to be concerned as to what is going on. The population is being dumbed down in order to create a slave population. Freedom and the prosperity that comes with it is quickly becoming non-existent. At the moment the only industry the American government openly has invested heavily is in the Armed forces. America or more accurately the corporation named the United States Inc. has military bases all over the planet, submarines that are nuclear powered and only need to re-fuel every 150 years and many other military installations of every possible type. Yet if can't seem to find the funding to upgrade schools in the country and especially in poverty stricken cities.

A laughable concept if it was not so sad and serious: The levels of ignorance in American schools breed violence, despondency and sadness in the hearts of the population. Then the medical profession issues and prescribes the only solution they have been allowed to learn, to prescribe psychiatric mind altering – organ destroying medication. Doctors of course have no other choice as the medical profession is taught within certain parameters of information. Holistic medicine is ridiculed in the mainstream as hocus pocus and lacking significant medical application. Some doctors will say some things in private to a patient that they will not publicly state for fear of losing their job. Natural cures exist for ailments but since doctors can't profit from them, they are not mentioned to patients. Instead a pill of synthetic base is given to patients regardless of the many potential side effects of such pills. Michael Moore in his film "Sicko" exposes the incompetence of the medical industry in America. Although superior care is available it is mostly reserved for the wealthy and sometimes not even then.

Chapter 15

Mind Control, Music, T.V. and it's Influence

All industries in America are shaped to operate and stay within certain limits. These limits are usually in written form and created by the top of the structure or implemented by the top people of the structure. Usually limits or guidelines of operation are given to the top of the structure for implementation onto the lower part of the structure. When they are not, the limits imposed on the operation of any agency, department, office, or entity by outside owners or financing parties, the limits are created by the entities top administrators themselves. Much of the activities of any such entity is governed by the effective influence that is suggested by the creators or controllers of such entities. Influence through words and monetary incentives combined are very powerful. The people that have created this state of slavery in America are very well versed in the art of mind control. People's minds are unfortunately easily controlled to think in certain ways. Government spends hundreds of millions of dollars a year on studies concerning the thought process of the mind. Even private studies by non-government agencies that study the mind end up selling the information to government entities, as all information is eventually for sale for the right price. Through advanced methods of mind control, influence, suggestion, hypnosis, subliminal mind programming, and other means the government employees have been brain washed and programmed into believing certain things. Peoples reality is shaped through these advanced methods and people turned into automatic reacting robots that do not consciously think before they act or speak. Without intentional deliberation people do and speak and perpetuate the desired outcome of the master controllers in position of slave masters. From very high up in the structure of government power, the stage is set and the reality of the country framed. Deep behind the curtains and layers of political bureaucracy, the domino effect is set into motion and it flows down the political structure until it finally is spewed forth onto the people in society.

Government entities are not the only outlets for this type of control and brainwashing. It can even be called by the less sounding insidious name such as "influence" or "suggestion", the outcome is the same. The shifting of people's thoughts, feelings and emotions to a desired mindset so politicians in government can do as they are told. The outcome desired by government policy is not always good for the people. Most of the policies set by government are unfortunately geared towards testing the people's acceptance of slavery type existence. Slavery is slavery no matter what label it operates under. In a book titled "The Behavioral Foundations of Public Policy" there is prime examples of how government policies in society are causing the exact problems they are supposed to be fixing. Or the policies are making the problems worse. Many government policies are detrimental to society, yet organizations still implement them without consciously evaluation the long term results or widespread effect of such policies. Once again because many people in government and other government funded organizations just behave in the politically correct accepted way. People have lost their ability to critically analyze and think for themselves due to the high level of "Influence" directed at society through many sources. Some are influenced through media, television, radio and others simply influenced by material and monetary gain. This allows people it is supposed to be servant to. The steady encroachment into individual people's lives is the most effective method employed against the people to remove their last taste of freedom.

In his book "Influence: Science and Practice" psychology professor Robert B. Cialdini cites and gives examples of the many tested and proven methods of influence employed on people to manufacture thoughts and behavior in people. People's consent is manufactured and fabricated through simple but very advanced methods of influence. The book speaks mostly in the content of selling products to people. The professor gives many examples of how people are convinced, mind controlled or influenced into certain behavior of acceptance and or cooperation. Most if not all of these methods of influence that the professor speaks of are not limited to application in the field of selling products or services. As anyone that reads the books fifth edition can clearly see how these methods of influence can very easily be applied to any scenario that requires people's cooperation or consent. There is even a couple studies concerning government entities, but make no mistake that government is not aware of or employing such methods of influence. Influence methods are mind control under a more believable label. The professor that wrote the book is obviously an expert in influence and has titled his book in a more politically correct and acceptable way. This of course is to remove the sinister or evil connotations of what it really is, advanced "mind control" technology.

Many if not all major corporations use such methods in advertising and marketing in order to raise their revenue and profits. Most will even have their own experts in house to study, research and further develop methods to influence people's minds to benefit of the corporation. These corporations generate a lot of money in the millions or up to hundreds of billions of dollars a year in profit therefore they have plenty of money available to pay for such research and implementation of these kinds of methods. Government agencies also implement methods of influence to achieve their goals of enslaving the people. In the book by Professor Robert B. Cialdini on the back cover there is a small paragraph that tells a little about the author. It is very interesting as it reveals not only that major corporations such as "IBM" and the "Mayo Clinic" are his clients that seek consultations on the power of influence, but so is "NATO" a quasi-government-military corporation posing as an entity with good intentions. It says Robert B. Cialdini gives frequent speeches on "The Power of Ethical Influence" to such organizations as NATO. This makes it clear that even armed forces on a global scale employ advanced methods of mind control to gain compliance and consent from people. The curious question is: Are these powerful methods of influences used in an ethical manner? It is very doubtful as NATO is a military armed organization that basically enforces policies through killing people to enforce corporation's best interest under the guise of securing peace. How ethical can it be to enforce policy through killing and bombing people into compliance?

We should not be so naïve as to think NATO a branch of the self-appointed world government is the only enslavement agency in use of advanced methods of influence and mind control. American government agencies use covert and overt methods of influence and have been using such methods for decades. There has been many times in history where mind control methods are used by government agents to accomplish and carry out an order from the top of the structure. There have even been specific instances where individuals were targeted, such as documented in the astonishing book called "Mind Control". Where a tool of influence most widely known as hypnosis was used to control people's minds and behavior and actually use them as mindless robots, activities ranging from simple couriers or documents to carrying out killings for undisclosed beneficiaries. The advanced methods of mind control are so effective that testimony under hypnosis is even allowed to be used as evidence in some criminal courts. As a matter of fact simple methods of influence are employed everyday by the criminal court system to gain convictions against people. But individuals although targeted for many odd reasons, are not isolated targets that occur rarely, these unknowing that without specific knowledge of these methods, it is pretty much unbelievable that they work.

Advertising in commercials on T.V. is a lesser form of mind control we can call strong influence. Advertising has such a strong effect that corporations routinely spend millions of dollars a year to promote products and services. Even political campaigns use advertising to persuade voters to their position on political issues. Television plays a huge every day in the constant shaping of people's lives, realities and opinions on issues. Advertising on television has many different levels of styles, from simple influence all the way to aggressive subliminal messages that are unseen by the naked eye but visible to the subconscious. If subliminal messages in television were not effective then there probably not are laws against such use. These laws are rarely enforced but there have been major corporations implication I such outlawed activity, although the media rarely covers such issues because of government censorship. Many people mistakenly believe government does not censor or significantly modify the mainstream media outlets in America. That practice is relegated to countries such as communist China or North Korea, is what this government would have us believe, when in fact American government practices censorship of media in the same level when it comes to mainstream television media. Of course the good thing in America is that many private people have took the initiative to start independent sources of news like magazines, internet radio and websites, private news organizations and the dissemination of information through other books and periodicals.

Television also allows for the widespread use of mind control methods such as "Hypnotism" or more specifically "Conversational Hypnosis". There are many countless books that document the amazing power of hypnosis. This powerful tool can literally turn people into mindless zombies that behave as they are programmed to behave. Hypnosis is so effective it has been documented to be able to change people's body's internal functions. There is many doctors' that ethically employ this tool for the benefit of people's health. This same tool can easily be used for any unethical use desired by government and its agents. At first government advertising known to be false was simply labeled as "propaganda". Now people have been steadily programmed to not even openly criticize the government or be looked at as a paranoid conspiracy theorist. Or even worst be classified and associated with anti-government groups or other labels of undesirable connotations. The suggestion of accusing the government of wrong doing is unpopular in this massively brain washed and mind controlled society.

America has turned into a passive dumbed –down society but it is not totally the people's independent fault. Ion the part of history, direct violence was employed to control the masses but nowadays that violence has been combined with advanced methods of influence and mind control. In these modern times the television is a weapon of war. A silent covert war is being waged through information and mind manipulation without people being aware of the conscious assault on them. Movies today are so influential in people's lives, attitudes and chance of lifestyle that it is very shocking to see the list of most popular movies today. People's lack of knowledge concerning the power of influence in movies is troubling as the lists of most popular movies are all violent in nature. The most popular movies have to do with constant violence of many different types. Men, women and children watch these movies and laugh at people's heads being blown off and chopped off. Video games that are the most popular and graphic advanced seem to be related to killing and military related themes. Government is constantly promoting why it is mandatory that it invade and drop bombs on foreign lands. The most prevalent topics and themes in mainstream news media newspapers are violent activities such as robberies, murders, death and the like. America has unfortunately become obsessed with violence and misery. Music plays the same role in society and massive amounts of society subscribe to the flavor and theme of violence, misery criminal activity and destruction. The good thing about music is that there is a more open possibility for choice by the individual. In movies, television shows and mainstream news it is there by default and there must be more of a conscious effort to avoid such exposure to the violent theme. Today there is even a president of the United States government named Barrack Obama that shamelessly associates himself with a celebrity rapper named Jay-Z. This association is on national television for promotion of his second election to office; this association by the president to a rapper that promotes criminal activity, violence and evil themes in his music is totally irresponsible by the president. These types of public associations give the impression to young youth that it is acceptable to listen to rapper Jay-Z's music. Subconsciously promoting certain type of behavior in today's society. Jay-Z is known to rap about guns, killing, gang membership, women being promiscuous and drug dealing; All topics that influence the people that listen to this music, influences that lead to such behavior that is detrimental to people in the community and the country as whole. Freedom of speech is of course priceless and a very fundamental right for anyone to express themselves in any manner they please and every freedom loving person should agree Jay-Z has this right. The fact that a very influential and public figure such as Barrack Obama should not promote behavior that is detrimental to our children and people in society is a responsibility that is obvious. President Barrack Obama is supposed to be a very educated and informed man, he obviously made a conscious choice to publicly associate himself with Jay-Z that promotes such detrimental behavior. The president of the United States is either very ignorant or an active participant in the creation of a slave country. He could just be mind controlled himself. Most likely it is intentional conscious behavior as he is a president with access to top secret and classified information of the most recent advanced mind influencing and mind controlling technology, or then again a man that is uninformed but believes he is highly educated, but is really easily controlled and duped was purposely installed as president of this American government to allow those slave masters behind the scenes to impose and advance their agenda.

What freedom loving people should concern them with is; what is the root causes of the slavery today? Why do people self-impose such enslavement behavior? Why is people's behavior so detrimental to our existence and advancement of freedom in light of such advanced knowledge and information available to the public? Why are our minds attracted to violent movies, video games with so much being mentally manipulated to believe we want such things? With psychology and the study of the mind so advanced there really is no excuse for the present mental and physical slavery to exist. The low standard of expectation from ourselves and people in our society is impregnated in people's minds through false thoughts by methods of influence, suggestion, hypnosis and mind control that make people stagnate and accept the current mental state of mankind.

Chapter 16

FEMA Camps, Citizen Camps

Not only is America in a state of slavery, it has been in a state of slavery for the last one hundred years if not longer. Freedom existed at some point in this land until government became too organized to influential and basically to big and more powerful than the people themselves. In 2013 the government is at a point where it has come to be just as any other dictatorship in history. Just as Adolf Hitler placed people in concentration camps, the American government is in position to do the same. The American government has acknowledged that it has detention centers in place called FEMA camps to detain citizens and others in case of civil unrest across the nation. These detention centers also known as citizen camps have been constructed all over the nation with railroads entering into them. Hitler did the same thing. Hitler disarmed the people through methods of influence and persuaded the population to give up its guns because they were unnecessary. The American government is at that stage. The president Barrack Obama and his administration actually challenged in court the 2nd Amendment to the constitution which is the people's right to bear arms. This happened in 2009 and the U.S. Supreme Court struck down the attempt, but for the government to even attempt such a thing speaks volumes of the government's plans and intentions for the future. Anyone can go on YouTube.com and see videos about these FEMA camps all over the nation. People make these videos and post on youtube.com out of concern for the deterioration of freedom in this country. Some people might be jumping to conclusions, but a critical analysis of these facilities does raise some important questions about what is going on and why the government would have concern of a mass civil unrest across the nation. It certainly is a big coincidence that citizen camps are being constructed all across the nation while at the same time the government through its puppet the president, is attempting to remove a constitutional right to bear arms that has been in place for over 200 years. These citizen camps are the American version of Hitler's concentration camps, designed for swift and mass incarceration of the people as evident by railroads leading into these places. There really is no reason for such facilities unless government was about to cause a scenario where people would protest on a a nationwide scale. The American population would not cause civil unrest on a nationwide scale for any trivial reason. At this point in time the American population is so trained to be passive and acceptant of government corruption, that it would take an event of never before seen proportion, to cause this nationwide civil unrest.

FEMA camps and such detention centers should not even be allowed to be constructed in a land of truly free people. In the event that government would consider such mass detentions, it only would reveal peoples lack of respect for government. Obviously proving the people do not truly consent to be governed therefore government would or should have no authority to mass incarcerate any so called free people. The government operates as a slave master and views the people as its slaves, or else it would not even contemplate such citizen camps. Government constantly creates laws without the people's consent to the point that any consent from the people has been rendered irrelevant and not required. Many people do not vote and have never registered to vote but still find themselves subject to rules made by unelected people. Representatives in government such as congress represent big money interest and or those that print dollar bills. After the mass incarceration in this country, if it ever happens, people will have only themselves to blame. In this country there is plenty of sources or information and opportunity to use this information to peacefully bring the true concept of freedom back to this land. Government should be kept in the position of servant by responsible people that are interested in true freedom, the future of people and interested in the advancement of mankind through peaceful informational revolutions, basically by spreading the information necessary to promote freedom responsibly. Any incarceration of the people in mass movement to any type of detention centers will not solve any issues for the better in the long run. All this would do is temporarily put on pause a problem. It would also continue the same old draconian and pre-historic concept of peoples existence, which is nothing more than modern day slavery with lofty labels and discreet implementation methods.

Chapter 17

Patriot Groups and Resistance

The lack of organizations that promote complete truth for the benefit of the peoples true freedom is a major problem. Today as of January in 2013 there is not enough groups of people interested in taking on such a task. Peaceful informational dissemination is the only solution to the current state of slavery that many accept as freedom. Violent revolution is something some people promote within freedom groups, but violence truly is not the ultimate solution. The only long term and most desirable solution to remove slavery as a concept of existence are to inform everyone as to the alternative and more desirable concepts. This war being waged against the people at the moment is on many fronts, but the most damaging to freedom and the most valuable to the slave masters is the people's lack of knowledge concerning every topic that manages people's behavior and thoughts. At the moment there is many concerned people in America that are spreading the information as to the constant deterioration of freedom in America. A real interesting individual is a man by the name of Alex Jones. This man runs an independent news website called www.infowars.com and exposes many important things happening in America. It's almost like a government watch dog type of group. This website does a great job of covering important topics that affect people's freedom in America. Many people in America have taken the initiative to develop some sort of news outlet or group that informs the general public with topics relating to freedom in America. Most of the times these type of activities are quickly labeled as ant-government movements. They are even labeled as patriot groups. A lot of these groups have some weird approaches or concepts as to what the problem or solution is to the current status of slavery in America. Some approach the issue with questionable legal theories and concepts. Like a site called www.creditorsincommerice.com. Then you have a website by Marc Stevens at www.marcstevens.net and many other similar sites with slightly different approaches to dealing with the American court system. Marc Stevens even wrote a book called "Adventures in Legal Land" that exposes the illusion of citizenship for what it really is, just modern day slavery. One of the most brazen attempts to remedy the issue of slavery in America is this group of people that claim to have created a new government alongside the current one. There is even a site this group has created for every state in the union. For example there is www.republicofcalifornia.org and this site claims to be a recruiting ground to join the newly formed government. So many different approaches to solving the dissatisfaction of the current government are being tried by many different people. All this shows is how unhappy Americans are with the current concept of government. There is obviously many people in America that feel this way and have attempted what they believe are a solution, whether they are right or wrong. At one running an organization named "Taking Back America". This organization attempted to exclude itself from membership in the current political society. Eventually the government agents filed for a court order to shut down the activities of this group. This group was labeled as a tax protester group and tax laws were the weapons used to shut down the informational distribution activities of the group. The amount of patriot groups in America are growing fast and consist of all races and people from different walks of life with the goal of preserving and exercising freedom.

Most politicians usually go along with what is politically correct to secure their political careers and monetary gains. Every so often there is a politician that attempts to speak out but they only last so long and can only do so much as one person. A few years ago a man named Jessie Ventura that was a famous professional wrestler ended up in politics. This man became the governor of Minnesota and eventually left his political position. After this job as politician, Jessie Ventura was even running a "conspiracy theory" type show for a while. Obviously something he saw or experienced in his position of governor made him look into conspiracy type theories in government. His experience in government had such a profound influence on him that he even wrote a popular book called "Don't Start the Revolution without Me". The title of that book pretty much sums up his opinion of his feelings concerning what is going on in politics and government today. There are many politicians that speak of their concern of where government is headed and of loss of peoples freedom. Too bad that is all they do, as most politicians that complain simply go along with what is politically correct and healthy for their career. At the end of the day politicians do what keeps the money coming their way. Talk with no action is worthless. By design of the system any politician that goes against the grain of enslaving the population further by the day, ends up removed from office, especially if the politician aims at key tools of enslavement. Such as trying to restore people rights or giving people more power over government. One good example is John F. Kennedy that publicly spoke out against wealthy secret societies in this country. President Kennedy as everyone knows was killed in public and many believe it was for his opposition to wealthy families controlling politics. There certainly have been many other politicians silenced through less violent and less public means.

There is supposed to be a militia in every state of the American union that is ready to defend the nation from foreign or "domestic" invasion and threats to the people's freedom. One website from a California Militia group claims on its site that it will defend the constitution and country from any physical invasion. This militia is really a joke, these members of militias will wait for an open physical invasion from a foreign or domestic source, but they will most likely never see it. In America there is an invasion that happened and is going on at this very moment, but it is an assault against the people through intellectual means, a silent war with no guns being fired.

Politicians pass laws to further enslave the people and no one is organizing an intellectual opposition to counter attack. The court system is corrupt and part of the enslavement tools currently keeping slavery in place. There must be an organized intellectual and peaceful move of a more effective method outside the corrupt court system. People must use their minds more creatively and effectively to actually find a remedy to the current status of modern day slavery in America. If not then when the politicians remove people's right to bear arms, then it will be too late to a peaceful approach to America's government of no consent. There will be many people in America that will rise up against the government and a revolution will mostly hurt the people more than government. People's refusal to recognize and use our minds as the most powerful tool for a peaceful and intellectual approach will keep people on a path to slavery and violence. Without people willing to be informed and knowledgeable of the laws, our political process, history, the monetary system and many other topics that determine our daily existence, people are doomed to always fall back into the same traps used throughout history to enslave a population.

Chapter 18

Conspiracy from within

At the moment America is on the brink of collapse in its economy and the nation is already in a state of modern day slavery. Government operates outside of its intended purpose and dictates from a position that implies superior status over the people. From critical research and analysis of the American government it would appear as though politician's actions are intentionally designed for the purpose of destroying America as a country and its concept of freedom. The freedom in America of people to live life on peaceful terms and of their own choosing is almost completely gone. Every year people's rights are legislated away or into restriction to reduce people to slaves and just out right for profit cattle, a conspiracy from within the American government exist at this present moment to crumble the fundamental structure of American government. Many would say the concept of America is already been tweaked to operate as a slave plantation with more rules and restrictions on people's rights than any time in history. Every year more laws are added to the books, some are opposed by the people but many are not. Thousands of new laws are passed every year and this is how government slowly tightens the rope around the people's necks. Raising taxes to the point where fifty percent or more of people's earnings go to many different types of fees, fines, or just outright income taxes. Many millionaires and billionaires more from state to state to wealthy people even have gone as far as leaving the country and giving up their citizenship to the corporate U.S. government.

While many people that love this country and claim to be quick to defend it wait and watch for a foreign source to attack it militarily, the politicians do the dirty work and pass laws that are attacking people's freedom, people's health through medicine and the food supply, the economy and the mental health of America through silent psychological warfare. This nation's people are under attack and the enemy hides in the position of government agents. Offices of government have been hijacked and conquered by the enemy of freedom. Money flows to the pockets of politicians through corporations created for the sole purpose of hiding the source of money. Most of the time there are two or three layers of corporations in place to shield the entity of these donors of money to politicians. Most politicians are members to secret societies and of fraternal orders that manipulate their thinking and position on political topics. Mostly it's a simply done through bribery involving material gains. Peer pressure also plays a role as these politicians a lot of the times owe their political career to these secret societies and its favors from brotherhoods. Politicians usually have an oath they took to these secret societies and then they go and take an oath to support the constitution of this country, most of the time with the oath they respect is the one to their secret society. A lot of the time the societies, brotherhoods, organizations, or groups they belong to are not very secret at all. Secret societies like "skull and bones" out of Yale University and the "Freemasons" are heavily involved in government and other positions of social engineering. These people have their mind controlled through bribery and mental manipulation within these societies. The members of these groups are exposed to ancient beliefs of magic, sorcery and many types of superstitions. Most if not all members become obsessed with the teachings of these groups and very understandably as members do reap rewards. The downfall is that these teachings mostly prevent members from evolving their mind further than acceptable by the mental parameters set by the organization. This whole process contributes to the slavery of mankind because these otherwise intelligent members become effectively neutralized from advancing their mental capacity and concepts that would collectively assist mankind in bettering our existence. Membership in these types of brotherhoods by male and female politicians does severely impact society and the advancement of mankind. It is not only politicians but also many people in position of corporations or think tanks and such organizations that partake in the design of society and the rules imposed on it. Even when rules or laws cannot be imposed on the people through apparent consent by elections, government has other legal loop holes that they use to impose their will on other people to further enslave the population. Elections where people vote can easily be rigged and manipulated to get a certain result, so results from elections a pretty much irrelevant. Fraud has been detected many times in elections in history just as recent as the George Bush scandal when up against Al Gore. With new computerized voting machines the fraud is easier to commit and virtually undetectable. With so many politicians, professors, experts, doctors, scientist, businessmen, and others in position of stature and influence so corruptly behaving or just ignorantly manipulated by these secret societies, there is little chance of any chance on its own initiative from within government. It must be independently thinking people from society that are not under influence, consciously or unconsciously, of any group forcing the agenda of slavery upon the people to take the initiative and change the current status of existence. Most importantly this change must be created through peaceful means in order to sustain the change and prevent society from reverting back to slavery. History has proven that when violence has been used to escape slavery and gain freedom, it is only a matter of time before the people are conquered again. The conquering in history usually comes from an outside source but times have changed and new methods are used to conquer people and render them slaves. Today as evident by laws passed by government, it is government agents working from within that are actively enslaving and conquering the people. These politicians put chains of slavery on their own posterity without realizing the future impact of their collective behavior with other politicians. Politicians every year dismantle piece by piece the so-called safeguards put in place by the constitution to protect people's freedom. All of congress and other politicians are guilty of usurping the legitimate role of government, if one ever actually existed.

The bottom line is that government is founded for the purpose of governing, controlling and basically enslaving another, if done with true consent of a man or woman that would be different, than the actual role of government today. But the current structure of government is destined to fail from within, because as it operates today a group of people calling themselves by fancy names such as judges, supreme courts, congress, legislatures and other names can simply agree to do something to any group or individual people and they do it and enforce it by violent force and even murder. Governments today call themselves republics, democracies, socialist, communist, kingdoms and names like that but it is an insult to people's intelligence that see them for what they really are. All are nothing more than mechanisms that allow for slavery to exist in different ways, but it clearly is slavery. When one group or individual can impose his will on another group or individual without the true consent of the other it is slavery, point blank. Currently it is accepted normal practice for government to kill people as they determine appropriate such as in a war where innocent non-involved civilians are killed and looked at as collateral damage. Entire town, schools, hospitals and other locations are blown up and innocent people killed because governments declare wars. These decisions are made by politicians from inside governments that send 18 and 19 year old kids off to kill and die in distant lands. People are manipulated to go kill and die for their country, but they fail to realize they are mere pawns in a chess game where death is real. This is why government sends recruiters to High Schools to convince kids that don't know any better to give up their lives for a government that will neglect their needs once they come back from war, if they ever come back alive.

The fix is in, and the conspiracy operates from within this American government to collapse the inner structure. The enslavement happened from within, and government waste no time in securing the chains of slavery even stronger everyday on the American people. For the majority of population the slavery is an accepted way of daily life. High taxes, high cost of living, fees, and licenses required for just about any business or profession are heavy weights on the average person's back. The majority of the population in America is not wealthy and is subject to constant pressure to maintain quality of life. Most of politicians in congress are wealthy and do not feel the daily pressure an average American does, but is themselves subject to one day become slaves overnight just like the average American. The wealthy must not see a problem with the current status of government concept and its operation, because if they did they would organize and do something about it. Since wealthy people have the financial means to help shape a better society and they don't, then one may think they are happy with the current status.

Chapter 19

<u>Wealthy Families</u>

Wealthy people in wealthy families in America do appear to be happy with the current status and concept of government because they do have a reason to be satisfied with the current status in this country. Wealthy people that live in this state of slavery in America enjoy more freedom than the non-wealthy. Having huge fortunes of money remove many restrictions that are placed on average Americans. The restrictions are still there but for the most part have little or no effect on the super wealthy. Five hundred dollar traffic tickets for speeding are no big deal and barely get recognition from the super wealthy. Many laws also don't apply to the super wealthy because they can afford to manipulate the legal system through super expensive lawyers that can beat charges or just flat out pay bribery cash over to judges, police, and prosecuting attorneys. Wealthy families or just wealthy people in general get away with murder a lot of the time. Not always, but a lot of the time. One of the best examples in recent times of wealthy people that manipulated the legal system with piles of money is O.J. Simpson. He was accused of a double murder and trial was even televised on national television. The evidence was overwhelming against him based on some evidence found by police, but there was no eye witness to the crime. He ended up getting a not guilty verdict and was released from jail. He might really be not guilty of the crime, but the point is that anyone accused of such a crime that does not have millions of dollars to put up a defense, would have easily got convicted. Another popular celebrity that pays to be exempt from the law is Lindsay Lohan; she is routinely in trouble with the law for many things such as cocaine possession, driving drunk and other accusations all while on probation for something. She has managed to pay bail and stay out of jail for the most part although she has spent some time in jail. Another wealthy woman name Paris Hilton was sent to jail for something and according to the Los Angeles Times Newspaper she was allowed to use a cell phone in jail and was given other benefits that regular inmates were not allowed.

The downside to what these wealthy families enjoy is that on a bigger scale they too will find themselves in undesirable situations if the current state of slavery does not change course. Some people are super wealthy like Steve Jobs, the owner of Apple computers, and even he found himself in a situation where the slave state status cut him short on life and his money couldn't and didn't help him. He died they say from cancer in his body somewhere. Cancer is a disease that exists and kills people on a regular basis because the current slave state restricts research and information into cures. Research and information concerning cancer and other diseases is only allowed to venture into controlled areas because of government guidelines and laws. Most research is done through government funding therefore it is easily controlled. Medical research is manipulated with many creative methods that result only in treatments for companies to make money from medicines but cures that solve the disease are not developed. In the case of Steve Jobs, he could not buy his life cure, at least not in America. His money bought him the best medical care in America but that was it, he was not able to buy the cure because of restrictions on information that would lead to it. Millions die every year, rich and poor.

Wealthy families for the most part are more likely to contribute to the continued enslavement of the people because they most likely financially gain from the current status. There is a class of wealthy families that are in a higher category. Such as the wealthy people that are entrenched deep in the functions of the government on setting rules and regulations concerning many topics, such wealthy families have a paid off representative in government congress or other high positions of influence. Some wealthy families even have a family member involved in the government. The Rockefeller families are one of those families that have a direct family member involved in government and they have many measures they implement for the financial gain of their family businesses. The Rockefeller family has more than one family member involved in government in high positions then they have also allies all throughout government positions that help them gain support for imposing anything they want.

There are many wealthy families that are in this higher category that financially gain through involvement in government. These families usually set up corporations of all different types to profit in astronomical amounts. This ensures that these families continue to have money to buy out politicians votes in order to perpetuate these huge financial gains. A lot of these wealthy families have been involved in government for 100 years or so, therefore the power and influence they wield is beyond strong. These type of families practically are the government and dictate the direction of government and the rest of the politicians just go along with the flow and act to set a rubber stamp on laws, policies, and regulations imposed.

All these wealthy families and individuals in the country do live a more free life than middle class or poor Americans, but they are still in jeopardy in the event the people of the nation one day actually gather and organize in a meaningful method to root out corruption and bring to justice any of these wealthy criminals. These wealthy criminals bank on the current criminal justice system to actually protect them through mock trials where judges control what juries hear as evidence, but these criminal courts might change in an instant overnight. Such as what is currently taking place in the U. K., where groups of average working middle class citizens are approaching the court houses and demanding the arrest of judges. People can only take so much corruption and the day Americans get to that point there is going to be a change in power and the structure of power. So for these wealthy families to continue to do what they do is very arrogant of them. Really it is mainly foolish for such behavior to continue, particularly in light of the current situation in America. Currently many Americans all over the country and across class lines are becoming pressed to the point where mental awareness is showing everyone the reality that Americans are slaves.

Higher and higher taxes are happening every year, harsher laws for petty offenses are being imposed,, corruption at all levels of government are to maintain control of population. The government combines those operations with the use of the state controlled media such as major television news stations.

Any failure by those wealthy families to analyze the current state of the country concerning a potentiol peaceful or violent outbreak by the general population , and to make a true assesment and preparation of it could ultimately render these wealthy families victims to a peacefulor violent change in the structure of the society. The wealthy individuals could just simply immediately leave the country for protection of a safer place , but that is if they get the chance or the warning of any such threat . Groups of people could band together overnight and just swarm factories , offices , and homes of these wealthy and not get a chance to run , or bribe anyone with their unlimited wealth . It's most likely that thse super wealthy individuals and families do not have a fear of such a thing happening , but that is only because of the fact that their super wealthy lifestyle keeps them out of touch from the general feeling of the population , and the fact that most of these wealthy families have been so for many generations , some sopanning over 200 years from the beginning of this country. All these facts do not change the reality of the situation about America today. America is in a state of slavery , of such deeply entrenched corruption in govenrment, and it is touching every class of people now that a huge portion of the population is aware of the problem. Rich and poor complain about our government incometence , about government overstepping it's legitmate purpose and the many other complaints that the people have. All It takes is for something or someone to take the lead and initiate a movement and if it happens at the right time in the right way then it could mean a world of change for the country. At the moment there is an informational and peaceful revolution happening in this country . At this moment in February of 2013 the president is pushing to remove the majority of guns from the law abiding citizens in this country . He said if congress will not approve his new laws then he will make them laws by issuing executive orders. These orders become laws instantly and are not subject to a vote. Basically the president is saying he will make laws as if he sees fit regaurdless if congress will not vote to pass them . It's like telling someone to give you their money or you will take it by force, either way it's robbery . These types of maneuvers by the government can cause the masses of people to come together and organize against the government .

What government fails to realize is that many in government positions in military, lawenforcement, and non-military but powerful positions will not agree to such tactics to dismantle what is left of the constitution , piece by piece.

Hopefully there is a peaceful approach to turning the tide of government encrochment on people's rights and lives. If not this whole country will unfortunately pay the price of a violent revolution and the infighting will defenitely change the current status of mostly peace that the country enjoys.

Chapter 20

The Solution

From the looks of things the government is pushing for the people to actually start a violent revolution , a civil war against the government in order for government to have the excuse to kill many people and remove the last of remaining freedoms people enjoy. Then the world government can step in to create a solid slave state through violence , basically taking people back in time to the dark ages in modern times where technology will be used to restrict people and information , reducing them to perfect slaves for the benefit of the few families that created without consent the world government . Just like ancient times thousands of years ago, there is a ruling class of families that is undisclosed to the public but is very much in control directing world development . Groups like the G20 that get together every year to talk about the development of the industry an all upcoming use of technologies , are the type of groups that are formed and run by wealthy elite that are in business of enslaving the general population.

For some odd reason these wealthy families and individuals obviously have encoded within their DNA the belief that they are superior and that it is their god-given right to hold down people and use them as they see fit. Much like and no different than the kings and the royal families position, that they are superior because of fate has provided them a superior station at birth or through a series of hard work, luck and determination to succeed and become superior. These wealthy individuals and many that work for them and seem to gravitate towards them., compassion and love for strangers and the human race as a whole is basically non-existant. As we analyze history and today , this type of attitude is prevalent in our capitalistic society. It is an unspoken acceptable truth in society and the business world , that compassion is not a profitable factor.

Thus, the only true solution to advancing people into a new dimension of freedom , prosperity , love , health , and abundance for all is for society as a whole and people as individuals to take the initiative to remove violent , corruption , dishonesty and greed from our approach to life. For if people attempt change of government corruption through violence then we are most likely to come in full circle to enslavement . We must come to the root of love for all , within our families and for the stranger. Not just in appearance of our actions but in true substance in our actions. For example people like Bill Gates and other wealthy celebrities are quick to donate 2 million dollars worth of vaccines for people in countries like Africa. On the surface it appears as if these are honorable actions with good intensions , but if we look at these actions deeper we are able to see the true purpose and effect . Why would Bill Gates an others claim to care and claim to want to help the sick people in Africa by providing medicines for these , but wont do anything to get the root of the problem . If 2 million dollars would be spent on drilling a water well , create a irrigation system , provide seeds for fruits and vegetables for the people in Africa then they would have a strong immune system to naturally prevent their bodies from contracting simple diseases like malaria that kill them . These wealthy people like Bill Gates know these things. When we investigate Bill Gates beliefs about world population , we see his true intensions . Bill Gates and big celebrities believe that world population is too high and we must stop the population growth because it threatens world peace somehow , they say. The world government claims the biggest threat to the human race today is over population . This position gives us an understanding why so many wars continue today. There are many government agencies that do studies and claim that over – population is the biggest threat to the world. These type of beliefs and other of limitations is what some use to justify to themselves the covert operations and methods employed by them to reduce the human population.

The solution is for overage people to unite and organize peaceful methods to rally up support from other people to speak up an make it be known to government agents of all types that things must change. These community and nationwide groups need to put together plans to remedy the numerous issues that face America today. People in America should let it be known that corruption will not be tolerated, nor poverty, unfair treatment of people, or many other methods of enslavement including suppression of advanced technology . The fact that government intentionally holds back advanced technology from the general population is totally unacceptable . Today there is many advanced medicines , electrical components , fuel technologies , natural cures and other superior methods of doing things that are held back from the general use of the population in order for the people to stay in a state of dependence on the government. These advanced technologies are also held back from the people in order for certain corporations to profit and maintain strongholds on industries. These monopolies on industries are artificially created by corporations getting government to pass laws to prohibit other from participating. Such things as prohibitive taxes, fees , or licenses are imposed requirements by government for no other reason than to exclude certain or most from any industry.

The oil industry is one of those industries that came to mind that easy to expose. Cars run on petroleum oil based gasoline for no other reason than because the oil industry pays off government and other agencies to continue prohibitive restrictions on the use of electricity or other renewable fuels all for the financial gain of the families like the Rockefellers that operate like criminal mafias. There is many alternative fuels that cars can run that's superior to oil: one good example is the hydrogen powered cars developed by Japan. This hydrogen car basically runs on water , yes , on water with no pollution to the environment. Electric cars are another example, some electric cars even have solar panels on the cars body to instantly recharge. The technology that is available today is futuristic and highly superior to what is in use in the mainstream in todays mainstream of society today. Greedy individuals in certain positions financially gain by suppressing technologies while the earth , community and society deteriorate and suffer unnecessarily. We must come up with a plan to distribute and implement better methods of living to raised the living standard for everyone , not just for some. This in turn will empower people to live healthier more abundant lives which foster love and compassion for the benefit of mankind. Many discoveries in history that have advanced mankind and technology in many fields have been made by the so-called "average" or non-wealthy individual.

Therefor the theory of only wealthy people or smart people with the certain DNA can create wonders for society , is totally bogus. By giving everyone the opportunity to live healthy, abundant, loving, peaceful, free lives, there is a huge chance as history has shown , that amazing discoveries will occur.

We must be willing to go where the future takes us even if it means the shifting of wealth and power. Change is something that most people fear are uncomfortable with , but we must proceed where progress takes us for the benefit of the mankind.

People need to take the initiative and appoint themselves leaders in any industry and and organize groups to bring the mainstream better methods of living that encourage advancement . Even if it means living longer and more people on the planet earth. With advancements in techonology we would not over populate the planet because we can travel to other earth like planets that we can inhabit. It just a matter of traveling there. Everyday we use amazing techonologies like cell phones , computers , wireless music earphones and other things that just 80 years ago did not exist . Life really is a magical place with few limits nowadays . Most limits are self-imposed by peoples beliefs and government restrictions.

People can unite and create a better educational system , better health care, better communities , a better government structure with more flexibility , a better justice system with education and opportunity in mind , a better and more honest monetary system to enrich people instead or drive the majority to poverty. There is many issues, categories, and industries that need to be addressed all at once to transform this nation. Then America can return to the position of being a beacon of light it once was and bring not just hope and illusion to the rest of the world , but bring true change, opportunity , and advancement to the entire planet . In every category of life there is room for major improvement not just small improvement. In food cultivating industries, clothing, building, and all areas imagineable there is currently techonology and methods that are superior and are not being utilized for the benefit and advancement of mankind. This means there is trmendous opportunity for all the people to get involved and make a differnce in America. We are all responsible for our future and have all the power and resources to make a change for the better . All we have to do is read this book do some independent research and thinking with a little bit of imagination and love for us all as people.

It is us that owe it to ourselves and the future generations to make a positive change to improve life. We must take the lead and improve our existence through peaceful creative methods. After all government here in America was supposed to be designed to be a servent of the people, so we must tell government of "We the People" and we should hold it to standard. We as people need to take the responsibility of improving or local community in as many ways as possible and encourage others to do the same, stting of a chain reaction all over the nation to encourage goodness for all. There is no excuse or reason why some parts of the inner cities are neglected by local government, when billions of dollars are available for other things. There is many abled bodies in every community and we must gather the courage , love and sense of responsibility to ourselves to live better. In return it will enrich our lives , give more opportunities to our children in ways we cant even imagine just like no one could of imagined a cellphone 500 years ago in ancient times. The opportunities, are endless and infinite , what we can imagine we can create .That is the bottom line , we have the power to create something better . The current status of slavery in America is absurd, ridiculous , and draconian in many ways. All we need to do is open the daily newspaper and read about the endless violence in communities , the daily stories of government corruption and incompetence and we can see something needs to be done.

 We as people need to bring about that change. Not from within government but from without by planning and creative thinking to peacefully correct the undesireable things of this country and restore our nature given freedom.

This country is one of the greatest countries in the world but we have allowed pollution of dictators, kings and queena and others that impose slavery to enter our realm of existance and way of life. It is time for peacefull people to use their mind and bring about freedom as our creator intended. Government is what we as people have allowed it to become and the best remedy is the spreading of the truth to the entire country .... That we demand freedom and that this government is a servant that answers to "We The People".

THE END